How to Start and Run a
Rescue

by Jennifer Williams, Ph.D.

PRIMEDIA Equine Network
Gaithersburg, MD

First Published in 2007 by PRIMEDIA Equine Network

PRIMEDIA Equine Network
656 Quince Orchard Road, #600
Gaithersburg, MD 20878
301-977-3900

VP, Group Publishing Director: Susan Harding
Editorial Director: Cathy Laws
Director, Product Marketing: Julie Beaulieu

Book Design: Lauryl Eddlemon Graphic Design
Editor: Lee Nudo
Front Cover Photo: Sharon Martin-Holm
Back Cover Photo of the Author: Wendy Forchione

Printed in China

Copyright © 2007 PRIMEDIA Enthusiast Publications, dba PRIMEDIA Equine Network

Order by calling 800-952-5813 or online at www.HorseBooksEtc.com

All rights reserved. No part of this publication may be produced or transmitted in any form or by any means, electronically or mechanically, including photocopying, recording, or by any information storage or retrieval system, without prior written permission from the publisher.

DISCLAIMER OF LIABILITY: The authors and publisher shall have neither liability nor responsibility to any person or entity with respect to any loss or damage caused or alleged to be caused directly or indirectly by the information contained in this book. While the book is as accurate as the authors can make it, there may be errors, omissions and inaccuracies.

ISBN 10: 1-929164-36-X
ISBN 13: 978-1-929164-36-3

Library of Congress Cataloging-in-Publication Data

Williams, Jennifer.
　How to start and run a rescue / Jennifer Williams.
　　p. cm.
　Includes index.
　ISBN-13: 978-1-929164-36-3
　1. Animal rescue--United States. 2. Animal welfare--United States. 3. Charity organization--United States--Management. 4. Nonprofit organizations--United States--Management. I. Title.
　HV4735.W65 2007
　636.08'32068--dc22
　　　　　　　　　　　　2007008701

*This book is dedicated to my husband,
Spencer Williams, and my parents Ralph and
Cindy Taylor and Sue and Jerry Wathen.
Without their support and love I could never
have founded and run two great rescues
or written this book.*

Contents

Introduction		7
CHAPTER 1	What Is Rescue?	11
CHAPTER 2	So You Want to Start a Rescue	19
CHAPTER 3	Get Organized	31
CHAPTER 4	Prepare Your Paperwork	43
CHAPTER 5	Recruitment and Retention of Volunteers	57
CHAPTER 6	Public Relations	69
CHAPTER 7	Get the Law on Your Side	87
CHAPTER 8	Fund-Raising	99
CHAPTER 9	The Value of Networking	127
CHAPTER 10	Create Community Support	137
CHAPTER 11	Keep Detailed Records	147
CHAPTER 12	Insurance	157
CHAPTER 13	How to Battle Burnout	167
CHAPTER 14	How to Assess Body Condition	177
CHAPTER 15	Countdown to Rescue	185
CHAPTER 16	Disaster Preparedness	199
CHAPTER 17	Develop an Adoption Program	211
CHAPTER 18	Dog and Cat Rescue	221
CHAPTER 19	Wildlife and Exotic-Animal Rescue	233
The Author's Story		243
Appendices		245

This book would not be possible without the help of many people. The members, volunteers, donors, and equines of both Lone Star Equine Rescue and Bluebonnet Equine Humane Society taught me to run a horse rescue and made both of those rescues possible. Spencer Williams, Jodi Luecke, and Valerie Taylor reviewed and edited chapters. Many rescuers gave me interviews, ideas, and quotes for the book. Thanks also to those who helped me gather the photographs that appear at the end of each chapter.

A final thanks to the book's editors, Lee Nudo and Primedia Equine Network Editorial Director Cathy Laws, and Julie Beaulieu, product marketing director of Primedia Equine Network, the publisher.

Introduction

I have known about the need for rescue since I was young. When I was eleven, I began taking riding lessons at a local barn. Before long, I dreamt of owning my own lesson stable. I wanted to purchase all of the horses at auction, rehabilitate and retrain them, and use them in my lesson programs. I thought I could sell the horses to my students and then go on to save more horses. After my first horse died when I was sixteen, I wrote to a rescue organization I found in a magazine and requested information about horses available for adoption. I joined the Colorado Horse Rescue at about the same time.

I did not become actively involved in rescue until the spring of 1998 when I found out that horses I had once cared for had been removed from their negligent owner. I looked for an organization to help the horses, but I could not find one anywhere in Texas. Using the Internet, I found other people in the state who were interested in getting involved in a rescue, and together we formed Lone Star Equine Rescue, Inc. (LSER) that fall. We had a lot of questions about how to create a nonprofit horse rescue. While we could find plenty of information on starting nonprofit organizations in general, we could not find anything specifically about starting or running a horse rescue, so we learned as we developed the organization.

During my time with the organization, LSER grew tremendously thanks to the support of excellent volunteers, officers, directors and donors. People who were interested in starting a rescue frequently contacted me so I decided to write this book to teach others not only how to start a rescue but also how to run one.

When I started working on the book, I did not know that my time with LSER was drawing to a close. However, the end of my time with LSER led to a new venture—Bluebonnet Equine Humane Society. I've used the information I gathered for this book to help Bluebonnet start down the path to becoming a world-class organization, and I hope this information can help you, too.

This book focuses on setting up a nonprofit horse or equine rescue, since that's where my expertise lies. However, similar paperwork is required to set up any other type of animal rescue, and many of the guidelines for running a rescue can be applied to running other animal-related nonprofits as well since many animal-related nonprofits share similar challenges. If you are considering doing "private rescue," this book can help you also since you'll run into similar problems as a nonprofit.

The book is divided into four sections:

1. Starting a Rescue – Chapters 1 – 4

The first section covers important topics to consider and research before starting a rescue, including whether or not you have the time and money to devote to a rescue, how you'll structure your organization, and what paperwork you will need to complete in order to set up a rescue.

2. Running a Rescue – Chapters 5 – 13

This section covers topics you need to familiarize yourself with if you will be running a rescue. You'll learn how to recruit and retain your volunteers, develop a public relations program, and build relationships with law enforcement and other local organizations. This section also covers fundraising, record management, and coping with burnout.

3. Care of Your Horses – Chapters 14 – 17

The third section includes topics on caring for horses and other equines in your rescue. These chapters include information such as how to use the Henneke Body Condition Scoring Chart and how to quarantine, rehabilitate, evaluate temperaments, and adopt out your horses.

4. Bonus section: Other Species – Chapters 18 – 19

This section gives information specific to dog, cat, exotic, and wildlife rescues.

I have successfully founded and run two rescue organizations. However I am not an attorney, financial planner, or accountant. If you have legal or financial questions or concerns in setting up your rescue, please contact an attorney or accountant who can assist you.

I hope that this book will be a valuable tool to anyone wanting to start a rescue organization as well as those organizations already in existence. Good luck in your rescue endeavors!

For more information — www.howtostartarescue.com

Jennifer Williams, Ph.D.
www.howtostartarescue.com

o n e

What IS Rescue?

The answer depends on whom you ask and the circumstances that prompted them to get involved.

RESCUE. The meaning of this word may seem like a strange place to begin this book, but, it's often a source of debate among rescuers. The Merriam-Webster Dictionary defines the word as follows: "to free from confinement, danger or evil; to take forcibly from custody; or to recover by force." It goes on to state that rescue "implies freeing from imminent danger by prompt or vigorous action." Using this as a basis, I define an equine rescue as an organization that works to save horses from danger. (*Note:* For the purposes of this book, I'll refer to "horses" and horse rescues, however, the term "equine" also includes donkeys, burros, and mules.) This is a broad definition under which many types of organizations can operate. Despite this, many rescue groups disagree with this simple definition, each believing the parameters of their individual rescue group demonstrate the right way to do it.

Some people argue that all legitimate rescues should be 501(c)(3), tax-exempt, nonprofit organizations. Others believe that rescues shouldn't

1 | What IS Rescue?

allow breeding or the sale of adopted horses by their new owners. And there are those who believe that purchasing horses from auctions, feedlots, or PMU ranchers isn't really "rescuing" them, or that donated or surrendered horses aren't really "rescue horses." For the purpose of this book, I consider a rescue to be any organization that saves horses from danger.

After all, rescues that purchase horses at auction, as well as from feedlots and PMU ranchers, often save them from going to slaughter. Rescues who accept donated or surrendered horses may save those horses from being neglected or taken to auction. And those rescues which work with law enforcement save horses from being neglected or abused.

So, by this simple, broad definition you can see that horses need rescue from almost limitless situations. Horses have come to the rescues I've worked with from many different circumstances, but they all shared one characteristic: If we did not take them, they would be in danger. For example:

- Doc, a six-year-old Thoroughbred gelding sent to auction, and possibly slaughter, when an illness left him unable to continue racing.
- Angel, a six-year-old mare sent to auction and headed to slaughter because she had lost her foal and bucked when ridden.
- Cody, an aged gelding who once taught college students to ride, found starving in a barn because he could no longer keep up.
- Peanut, an adorable pinto pony in his 30s, found starving in a field. He required additional feed because of his advanced age, but his owners didn't want to provide it for him.

All these horses were lucky to find their way to a rescue that "rehabilitated" them (or restored them to health) and found them loving homes.

But horses are rescued for many reasons that aren't as clear-cut as those I mentioned above or those seen on Animal Planet. Neglected horses sometimes have to be rescued from the court system: Gaia, a three-month-old filly, and Athena, a yearling filly, were both emaciated when a law-enforcement officer discovered them in a dirt lot with no food. The courts removed the fillies from their owner, along with 15 other horses, but then ordered the sheriff's office to sell them at a local auction. The horses were then at risk of being purchased by "killer buyers" (those who purchase horses for slaughter), so a rescue group purchased them. Fortunately, the courts often award custody of neglected horses directly to rescue groups.

Horses are also rescued from potentially dangerous circumstances: Sometimes divorce, loss of a job, or an impending move forces an owner to sell or give away his horse. What's wrong with that, you ask? Horses that are advertised or sold at auction too cheaply (less than the price of horsemeat), and those offered as "free to a good home," are at risk of going to slaughter. Killer buyers will often pose as caring folks looking for horses for their children, grandchildren, wives, etc. Rescues often take in these horses to remove them from this danger.

The Many Faces of Rescue

Twenty years ago, horse rescues were much less common than they are today. There were a few organizations, such as the Hooved Animal Humane Society of Woodstock, Illinois, and Days End Farm of Lisbon, Maryland, that worked with law-enforcement agencies. There were also a few horse sanctuaries in existence, such as the Black Beauty Ranch of Murchison, Texas. The only way people heard anything about these groups was if they were involved in a publicized seizure of horses. Today, though, horse rescues are more common, and most horse owners and enthusiasts have at least heard of rescue cases, and many donate time or money to support such groups.

In recent years, countless horse rescues have sprung up across the country. Some operate only in specific geographic regions, while others are more far-reaching, such as South Carolina Awareness and Rescue of Equines, which attempts to cover an entire state, or Bluebonnet Equine Humane Society, which operates in multiple states (Arkansas and Texas, with plans to expand into other states). There are even organizations attempting to save horses across the nation.

Some rescues serve only a specific breed or type of horse. These include the Thoroughbred Retirement Foundation, which works to place retired Thoroughbreds in good homes across the country; and the Standardbred Retirement Foundation, which focuses on placing retired trotters and pacers. PMU foal rescues came into being to find homes for the foals produced as byproducts of the Premarin industry. (*Note:* PMU stands for Pregnant Mare Urine. To produce Premarin, which is used in female hormone-replacement therapy, mares must produce a foal every year to maintain sufficient hormone levels in their urine.)

Other rescues, such as True Innocents Equine Rescue in California, work to get horses out of feedlots, which are often used to hold them before they're sent to slaughter. There are also many rescues that open their doors to any needy equines, from Miniature Horses and donkeys to draft horses and mammoth mules. While their policies and methods of operation vary, all these groups have one common goal: to improve the lives of equines who are unwanted or neglected. These organizations are invaluable, as they help re-home and rehabilitate thousands of equines in need.

Where There's a Need, There's a Way

Animals in need of rescue have always existed, so why the increased number of rescues in recent years? There are many factors involved, but the two most influential are:

- *The Internet:* Hundreds of Web sites that discuss the need for rescue, outline how to get involved, and provide lists of horses available for adoption have sprung into existence. These Web sites also describe specific neglect cases and display numerous graphic photos of seized horses. After reading these stories, many people are moved to donate time and/or money, and to become involved in spreading the word about rescue efforts.

- *Law-enforcement awareness:* Law-enforcement officers have become more involved in investigating equine neglect and cruelty cases. There's often increased media coverage in horse-neglect cases, especially those cases involving severely emaciated horses, or cases in which large numbers of horses are seized from one owner. These high-profile cases prompt many people to join a specific rescue so they can assist law enforcement and help rehabilitate the neglected and abused equines.

There are many reasons why you might decide to set up your own organization rather than join an existing group. Maybe there are no rescue groups in your area, or your local organization is limited in scope (e.g., it takes in only certain breeds or horses from specific circumstances). Maybe you disagree with their operating procedures (e.g., they allow rescued mares to be bred), or perhaps they simply don't have adequate space for the number of horses in need, and you do.

To give you some other ideas, here are a few stories about people who formed their own rescues for a variety of reasons.

Valerie O'Brien of Fableview Equine Rescue, Missouri. Valerie grew up dreaming of running a no-kill dog rescue and sanctuary, but those plans were put on the back burner because the facility she dreamed of was far too expensive. Then she went to an auction with a friend, where she met an abused, skinny palomino who continued to haunt her. She decided she wanted to do something to help horses like the one she couldn't stop thinking about. Unfortunately, she lost her job, and life's pressing issues pushed her dreams of rescue further into the background. Then one night it came back to her—horse rescue was what she had to do, and her journey began. Valerie has since told me that when rescue becomes frustrating, she remembers the sad, unnamed palomino, and his memory keeps her going.

1 | *What IS Rescue?*

Kathleen and Allan Schwartz of Days End Farm Horse Rescue, Maryland. Toby was a friendly horse who lived at the same boarding facility where Kathleen and Allan boarded their horses. The couple noticed that Toby had started losing weight and his health was declining. Kathy and Allan became increasingly worried about him, so they offered to take him off his owner's hands. When Toby's owner consented and he came to Kathy and Allan, the gelding was hundreds of pounds underweight and too weak to get up after lying down. Because of the care and attention Toby received, he not only recuperated, but also formed a strong bond with his caretakers—one that prompted them to form their rescue. Toby became the first of thousands of horses that have since come to Days End Farm.

Chance's Miniature Horse Rescue (CMHR), a network of foster homes spread throughout the US. A Miniature Horse named Chance united an entire Internet community. It began with a message left on a bulletin board, describing a paralyzed Miniature colt that needed a new home. Several members on the bulletin board joined together to help the colt. Within three days of the initial message, Chance was in his new home. Unfortunately, his injuries were too severe, and his new caregivers couldn't help him.

Although Chance lost his life because of neglect, his story united the online Miniature Horse community, and they banded together to form Chance's Miniature Horse Rescue (CMHR). Within weeks of his death, CMHR formed and established a board of directors and officers, and began working on policies, procedures, and IRS paperwork. That one tiny horse prompted the formation of an organization that may help hundreds of other Miniature Horses.

AnnMarie Cross of Crosswinds Equine Rescue, Inc., Illinois. While working at a therapeutic riding school, AnnMarie met a mare that had been badly abused. So badly, in fact, that she'd risk injury trying to escape if any man approached her stall. After AnnMarie worked with her for just six months, the mare's confidence in mankind was restored and she went on to become a college-aged boy's beloved polo pony. After experiencing the mare's drastic turnaround, AnnMarie felt a need to become more involved in rehabilitating needy horses. Fifteen years later she formed Crosswinds Equine Rescue in memory of that mare.

Gina Brown of Spring Hill Horse Rescue, Vermont. Gina used to attend horse auctions for fun, not realizing that the unwilling participants in her "entertainment" were often sold to buyers who took them to be slaughtered. When she learned about the fate of many of these horses, she was horrified. She also learned about the PMU industry and its byproducts—the foals that so often end up in slaughterhouses. These two factors, combined with a growing dislike for the harsh training methods used in some competitive equine sports, prompted Gina and her family to begin a horse rescue.

Jeannie and Kenneth Holland of Casey Creek Horse Rescue and Adoption, Inc., Kentucky. A general love of horses and a desire to right the injustices they suffered prompted Jeannie and Kenneth to start their own rescue. They felt they needed to create a rescue to fill a very special niche—the unwanted foals from "nurse mare farms." These farms breed mares, then remove their foals shortly after birth so their dams can nurse a more expensive, well-bred foal that lost his mother to death or a prosperous race or show career. Until Casey Creek Horse Rescue and Adoption came along, these foals faced uncertain fates.

Their exact reasons aside, all these people have a few things in common: All possess a deep love for horses; they're all concerned for the welfare of horses; and many of them experienced a turning point—a moment when helping horses became one of the most important things in their lives.

Chance

Chance's first birthday was a celebration—a second chance at life. That is the day he arrived at the rescue. His owner had been reported for neglect, and it was clear that Chance had been hungry for most of his short life. His owner had too many horses, too little land, and not enough money. She finally realized she was in over her head and offered to give Chance away. One of our members took Chance and placed him with the rescue.

The day Chance arrived was the first day he'd been handled much by humans, and it was also his first day away from his mother. His birthday might not have looked bright to Chance, but it was a turning point for him. Up until this day he'd only known the pangs of hunger; what he didn't know was that such discomfort would quickly become a distant memory.

When he arrived at his foster home, he found plenty of fresh hay and clean water, and other young horses to play with. As Chance slowly gained weight he learned that humans brought food and they scratched his itchy spots. He also learned to lead, load in a trailer, have his feet handled, and stand for grooming. And he learned to enjoy being with humans.

Chance is now happy and healthy, and he loves all the attention he receives from his handlers. He's a lucky colt.

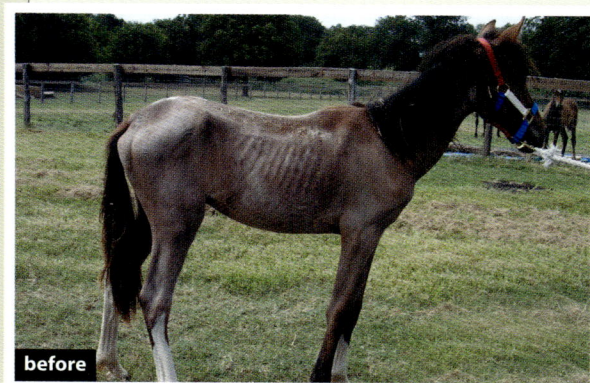

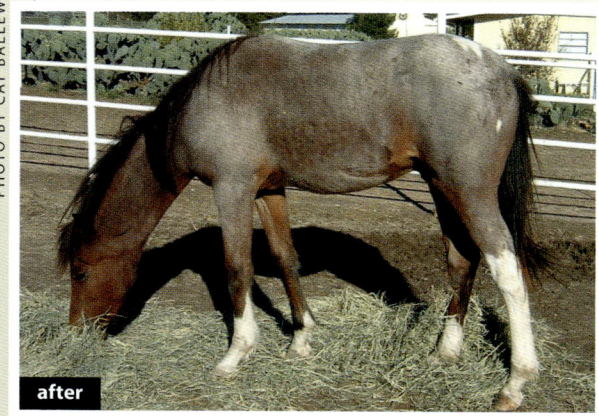

PHOTO BY JOANNE TERRY

before

PHOTO BY CAT BALLEW

after

two

So You Want to Start a Rescue

Get ready to change your life!

If you're seriously thinking about starting a rescue, there are many important issues for you to consider before you begin organizing it, putting together the necessary paperwork, and recruiting volunteers—topics that I'll cover in upcoming chapters. First, I want to warn you about the many demands rescue can place on your life.

Up-Front Costs

When you start a rescue organization, you'll have to provide most, if not all, of the start-up money. There's very little funding available for establishing rescues, and many donors won't support an organization that hasn't at least filed paperwork to become nonprofit. In general, donors prefer to support organizations with a track record, and will want to wait a few years to watch your progress. Your friends and family may be willing and able to provide some of the start-up money, but you'll need to pull together enough to set up the organization and begin caring for any horses your rescue acquires while you're wading through government procedures.

Some people get involved in rescue hoping they'll make money. They may want to fund their personal horse activities, or perhaps they want to quit their day job. You might think nothing sounds better than spending all your time doing rescue work and being paid for it. Unfortunately, it's hard to make money while doing rescue. As previously mentioned, start-up requires a substantial amount of money, and it typically takes several years to build the organization to the point of being able to allocate basic responsibilities to other members or volunteers, thus freeing you up to seek larger sources of income to maintain the rescue.

Many rescue organizations are set up to be run entirely by volunteers, with no paid positions at all. Rescues often have a difficult time making enough money just to feed their horses. Any additional monies that might

Expert's Tip

Valerie O'Brien, of Fableview Equine Rescue, believes funding should be your most important consideration. Many would-be rescuers fail to consider the expenses that rescuing horses entails. When you budget for rehabilitating an emaciated horse, or one that's ill or injured, first consider how much it costs per month to maintain a healthy horse, then plan on spending three to four times that much. Expensive surgeries and aftercare can drive the cost of rehabilitation even higher.

Valerie adds that she'd rather tell someone she can't take in his horse than overextend herself. Sound uncaring? Not when you consider that doing so could lead to the financial collapse of your rescue, and the inability to help any horses at all. If you're personally financing the rescue, overextending yourself can lead not only to personal debts, but also bankruptcy.

come in have to go towards promoting the rescue, improving its facility, or rescuing additional horses. Those groups that do have paid employees often have been around for several years.

Case in point: Lone Star Equine Rescue, Inc. was founded in late 1998 and didn't add any paid employees until 2003, and then its two employees were paid a very small stipend. One fulfilled the job of executive director, with responsibilities that included filling in for any volunteers unable to perform their duties; sitting on all committees; reviewing monthly officer and staff activity reports; assisting with public relations, fund-raising, and educational opportunities. Additionally, the executive director was involved in organizing seizures of neglected horses, working with law enforcement and county officials, preparing court cases, and testifying in court.

Lone Star's second paid employee was in charge of overseeing the rescue's horses. Her responsibilities included placing them into foster homes and relocating them if the placement didn't work out; maintaining contact with adopters to get updates on their horses; approving routine veterinary visits; obtaining approval for additional veterinary treatments from the rescue's officers; and overseeing the adoption program, which included deciding when horses were ready for adoption and then helping to set their adoption fees. She also worked with potential adopters and followed up on adopted horses.

Case in point: Turtle Rock Rescue of New Hampshire has one full-time and one part-time employee on its payroll. Although this rescue ran for its first six months without a paid employee, that farm had more than 50 horses, so the group had to hire help quickly. The first employee, who was initially part-time, helped to care for the horses; the position was changed to full-time when more funds became available. The rescue added another part-time employee a few years later.

The bottom line is, you need to examine your own finances and

2 | *So You Want to Start a Rescue*

determine whether you can commit thousands of dollars to your rescue, and be comfortable with the likelihood that it'll never be repaid. You need to understand and accept that it may take years for your organization to support a paying position—and it may never be able to do so. Few rescues are lucky enough to have even a part-time paid employee within the first several years.

The Time Commitment

The next thing to consider when you contemplate founding a rescue is how much time you can commit. In the very beginning, you'll be doing all of the work. At the very least, this may include caring for the animals, maintaining paperwork, and checking out potential adoptive homes. Depending on the structure of your rescue, it may also include recruiting foster homes, advertising and promoting your group, fund-raising, and much more. Over time, you'll recruit volunteers who can help share the work, but as founder of the organization, you need to be prepared to put in 40 to 60+ hours a week in the beginning.

Case in point: Becky Montanya, of Whidbey Island Rescue for Equines (WIRE) in Washington state, says she spends more than 40 hours per week working for the rescue. For her, this is an unpaid job, and since she has very few volunteers, most of the work falls on her shoulders. She's responsible for all the feeding and watering, training and exercising, and cleaning and maintenance on the farm; all fund-raising; maintaining the bank account; and issuing receipts for donations. She also recruits donations of feed, hay, and equipment; secures opportunities for public relations; and answers the telephone, e-mails, and correspondence.

Becky is constantly seeking new volunteers to help run the rescue, but as soon as she manages to offload one job, she quickly finds something else she can do to strengthen and promote her rescue organization.

Case in point: Gina Brown, of Spring Hill Horse Rescue, says the actual chores (e.g., cleaning, feeding, and treating injured horses) only require about four hours of her time per day, but the other miscellaneous tasks easily consume all the rest of her time. She and her family spend most of their evenings and weekends working on their rescue facility, and during the day she's busy answering the phone, revising policies, forms and contracts, keeping the books, and organizing fund-raisers and public-relations activities. In her words: "It seems like we eat, drink, and sleep horse-rescue stuff—it's definitely not a side-thing or hobby."

Lack of Privacy

Rescue work can be very invasive. Your phone may ring at all hours with requests for information about your group, for horses to be taken into rescue, and to file complaints of neglect. The weekends will be especially busy with phone calls, neglect cases to investigate, and people to meet. Holidays aren't exempt from phone calls, either. If you establish a foster-home program, a cell phone is a must so your foster homes can reach you in case of an emergency. You'll also need to make phone calls during business hours to veterinarians, law-enforcement officers, shelters and humane societies, and to solicit donations.

What About Your "Day Job"?

The needs of your rescue won't conveniently cease when it's time for you go to work, either. You'll need to take time off to attend court, pick up horses, and take them to veterinary appointments. You'll also need to be able to make, and take, phone calls during the day. If you have an understanding boss who supports your rescue work, your life will be easier than if you have to try to hide your "extracurricular" activities.

Some fortunate rescuers have bosses that allow them to make copies at work for cost, to accept phone calls regarding the rescue, and give them flex time so they can handle their rescue duties. Others, however, aren't so accommodating and may make it difficult for you to maintain both your work and rescue responsibilities.

Family Support

How your family feels about your involvement in rescue is critical. While you may be willing to sacrifice family vacations, nights out to dinner or the movies, and other luxuries, these decisions need to be discussed with your entire family. Do you have enough time to split between your children and the many horses that may pass through your doors, not to mention donors, adopters, and fosters who'll need your time and attention? Are your kids and your spouse willing to participate in fund-raisers, fostering, public-relation events, and other time-consuming activities?

Now's the time to talk to them honestly about what rescue will entail. Explain that while they'll have a chance to make a drastic difference in the lives of many animals, they also may have to give up vacations, put up with the phone constantly ringing, and get along without you when you need to spend time caring for additional horses and performing other rescue activities.

Case in point: Randy and Susan Morgan, of Painted Promises Ranch–Miniature Equine Rescue in Arizona, run a private equine rescue on their ranch. It's a family-run endeavor in which everyone is involved. The kids feed, clean up after, and exercise the horses that come into their rescue program. Randy runs errands and does maintenance, and Susan recruits donations, answers phone calls, and maintains their Web page. They all attend auctions together where they purchase horses they believe can be rehabilitated and re-homed.

Case in point: Becky Montanya, of Whidbey Island Rescue for Equines, is blessed with a supportive family. Her husband helps build the fencing and shelters for their rescue horses; her dad, sisters, and in-laws all assist with fund-raisers and other activities. And the emotional support they also offer is invaluable.

Case in point: Gina Brown, of Spring Hill Horse Rescue, also makes rescue a family affair. Her entire family works on maintaining the rescue facility. Her husband is often up mowing and cutting hay in the mornings before he goes to work, while her nine-year-old daughter helps out where she can. Gina admits that the rescue does put a strain on the family. Her husband rarely gets to ride the motorcycles he loves, and he even sold one so the rescue could purchase a horse trailer. Her daughter is sometimes jealous of the time her mom spends with the horses, but Gina says her daughter has become much more compassionate and nurturing now, and seems to appreciate the things she has much more then she used to. While rescue can be hard on their entire family, they're all involved, and they've learned to appreciate better the material things they can afford.

Even if you ultimately decide not to start your own rescue, it's a good idea to talk to your family about any rescue involvement. Fostering for a rescue, or doing any other volunteer work, can take money out of your pocket and time away from your family.

Case in point: Anne Herrin is a mother of three young girls and was a foster home for Lone Star Equine Rescue. She used the fostering experience to teach her girls about compassion and care for others. She told her children that they provided care for horses that no one else wanted. Her seven-year-old daughter, Hailey, became so involved in the fostering process that she took photos to school and told the other students about the rescue and how much it helped improve the horses' lives.

You'll need the support of your family and friends—not just their help with chores or involvement in the rescue's functions, but also their emotional support. Rescue can be emotionally draining.

> **Expert's Tip**
>
> **When asked what advice she would give to new rescuers, Susan Morgan, of Painted Promises Ranch—Miniature Equine Rescue, responded: "Make sure you're ready to handle the bad things that'll happen, because although you hope to help them all, there are some that you just don't get your hands on in time. You need to learn to get past the sorrow and/or channel it toward educating the public. And it always helps to concentrate on the success stories."**

The Emotional Toll

Often overlooked are the intense emotions that come with rescue. You'll undoubtedly encounter situations where you're simply too late. You need to ask yourself (and be honest) whether you would be able to let go of the horses that are beyond help. Each year, many people leave rescue because they can't do this and become overwhelmed by their emotions. They can't cope with the pain they feel for each lost animal, and they often think there must have been more they could have done. They feel guilty and end up unable to continue their rescue work.

In some cases the inability to let go can increase an animal's suffering. This happens when the person running the rescue won't, or can't, make the call to euthanize an animal.

My Experience

When I got involved in rescue, I had no idea what demands rescue work would make on my time, money, and family. All I knew was that I wanted to help horses—and I've learned the rest about rescues as I went along. I was lucky that Lone Star Equine Rescue began with 25 "charter members" who were available to split the work. However, for the first two years Lone Star existed,

I attended almost every event in which the group participated. This included fund-raisers, booths to promote the rescue, newspaper interviews, and more. I did most of the pre-adoption and pre-foster inspections and follow-ups, in addition to being responsible for every aspect of the organization. I also had to pay for most of the rescue's expenses up front, and got reimbursed when the rescue could afford it—often three or more months later.

The phone line for the rescue ran into our house for several years, and we often got calls early in the morning and very late at night. I carried a cell phone with me so our foster homes and officers could reach me any time, anywhere.

And whenever I went on vacation, I was "on call" with Lone Star and left alternate numbers where I could be reached.

Over time the rescue grew to where we had many volunteers who helped cover a wide variety of areas. But I was still very involved, spending more time each week working on rescue than most people spent on their regular jobs! Now that I've begun again with Bluebonnet Equine Humane Society, I know there'll be a huge demand on my time. I'm lucky because my husband

Expert's Tip

Valerie O'Brien, of Fableview Equine Rescue in Missouri, warns all potential rescuers about the emotions that are a natural part of rescue work. Sorrow or disgust can overwhelm you when a horse comes to you ill, injured, or emaciated. You may be shocked when you assist in a seizure of animals and witness firsthand the horror that humans can bring upon them. You may get angry with careless owners who don't feed their animals or cast them aside once they're no longer "useful." You'll have to learn to cope with these wide-ranging emotions without breaking down. To be able to do beneficial rescue work and to be taken seriously by others in your community, you must be calm and professional.

supports my drive to rescue, but it can still put a strain on our relationship. We set aside nights to go out to eat, see a movie, and avoid rescue work. And I schedule evenings where I don't answer the phone or read e-mail—always with the exception of emergencies.

If you've considered all these issues and still have the desire to start an equine rescue, consider first volunteering with an established organization. Be up-front and tell them you're volunteering because you're thinking about forming your own rescue, and would like to get some firsthand experience. You'll learn about how rescues are run, and you may learn things you can improve upon or things you hadn't yet considered.

After a period of volunteer work, you may decide against starting your own rescue and opt to continue volunteering. But if not, your next task will be to determine how you'll design your rescue program.

SUMMARY OF POINTS TO CONSIDER BEFORE YOU COMMIT TO STARTING A RESCUE:

- ❏ Can you commit enough funds for start-up costs and operation of the rescue in the beginning—with little hope of being reimbursed?
- ❏ Can you commit enough time to successfully run the rescue?
- ❏ Can you tolerate the invasiveness of rescue? (For example, phone calls early in the morning, late at night, and on weekends; and the need to carry a cell phone for emergencies, etc.)
- ❏ If you have a "day job," will your boss tolerate you taking time off and being interrupted by your rescue responsibilities?
- ❏ Will your family support your desire to run a rescue?
- ❏ Are you prepared to handle the intense emotions rescue can invoke?
- ❏ Can you let go of those animals that are beyond your help?

Rose

Although she was emaciated, Rose was one of the lucky horses in her herd—several had died before the rescue learned of their plight. Rose didn't trust humans when she arrived at the rescue, and she warily watched her caretakers from a corner of her pen. Over time, she seemed to realize that her caretakers wanted to help her and she slowly became more interested in them.

As Rose gained weight, her foster mom was concerned that she might be pregnant because her belly grew rounder much faster than the rest of her body! An ultrasound confirmed her foster mom's suspicions and we prepared to welcome the rescue's first foal. (Although we don't allow the breeding of our rescued horses or donkeys, we don't abort those who arrive at the rescue pregnant.) There was a dead donkey jack on the property from which Rose was seized, but her former owner said he'd bought her at an auction, so we didn't know if we would have a horse foal or a mule foal.

We also didn't know when Rose was due. The rescue ran a "name

before

PHOTO BY JENNIFER WILLIAMS

the foal" contest. Contestants guessed the foaling date, the foal's sex, and whether he or she would have long (mule) ears or short (horse) ears. The contestant with the closest date would get to name the foal. In the event of a tie, the contestant who'd guessed the correct sex and ear length would win.

Possible foaling days came and went, and the contestants rooted for Rose to foal on their selected day—but there was no foal! Finally one morning, eight months after her rescue, Rose's foster dad went outside to feed the horses, and he found a tiny mule colt in Rose's stall that looked to be only minutes old. Before long, Rockefeller—as the contest winner named him—was standing at Rose's side and she proved to be an attentive mom. Rocky was a perfect foal—and neither he nor Rose suffered any long-term effects from Rose's months of starvation.

PHOTO BY WENDY TAYLOR

after

three

Get Organized

Take the time to tend to some important details before you're tempted to leap into action.

At this point, you've thought it over and concluded that you can commit the time and money, and your family and boss will support your desire to rescue horses. Your next step is to create a vision for this endeavor—a precise plan for exactly what you want your rescue to do, including how you'd like to see it develop. So many rescue founders forget this important step, and as a result their groups struggle to define themselves and lack direction as they grow. You'll avoid this pitfall if you formulate goals for your first five years of operation, then consider what you'd like to accomplish even further into the future—10, 15, 20, or more years later. Once you've defined your vision, you can use it to help set up the rescue's structure, starting with the type of organization you want to run—nonprofit or private; sanctuary or "traditional" rescue with an adoption program. Then, among other things (which we'll cover here), you must determine what types of horses your rescue will take in, and how you'll provide for their long-term care and placement. The answers to all these questions will govern how you put your paperwork together (which I'll cover in Chapter 4), who should serve on your board of directors, and the officers and key volunteers you'll need.

If you already have a group of people interested in helping you form your rescue, schedule a series of meetings to determine how you'll proceed. If you'll be the only one working on the rescue in the beginning, you need to decide how you want to operate it so you can present cohesive plans to potential board members and officers.

Will it be Nonprofit or Private?

This is a big decision, and there are advantages and disadvantages to both types of rescue. Let's take a look at each one.

- **Nonprofit rescue.** Organizations that qualify to receive tax-deductible donations are given the designation of (501(c)(3) by the IRS. Many donors prefer to make tax-deductible donations, and they can only do so with 501(c)(3) organizations. Foundations that give out grant money will only award these dollars to organizations with 501(c)(3) status. So if you'll need to seek outside funding for your rescue, then you should consider a nonprofit structure.

The ability to solicit outside funding doesn't come without a downside, though. A 501(c)(3) organization is required to maintain accurate records, and to make them available to the public upon request.

- **Private rescue.** If you can fund the rescue yourself, without any outside sources of income, you don't need—and won't qualify for—501(c)(3) status. Some individuals who decide to get involved in rescue don't want the hassle of keeping paperwork and maintaining open books, so they opt for a private rescue.

The downside of running a private rescue is that income made from the sale or adoption of horses, or any other rescue-related items, may be considered personal income, which you'll be required to report and pay taxes on.

Sanctuary or Rescue

Another important consideration is whether you want to run a rescue program where the equines are eventually placed up for adoption, or a sanctuary where they come to live out the rest of their lives.

- ***Sanctuary.*** There are several advantages to running a sanctuary: You don't need to seek adoptive homes, and you don't run the risk of putting your horses into bad homes, hence you'll never have to worry about where your horses go.

On the other hand, there are several drawbacks to this type of setup. A sanctuary requires a lot of land and a strong fund-raising program as you'll be committing to years of care for each horse. Also, the number of horses you'll be able to take in will be limited by your space and finances. Once you've reached your maximum number of horses, you'll have to turn down all others until there's more room in the program, which usually occurs when one of the sanctuary's residents dies.

- ***Rescue with an adoption program.*** The goal of this type of program is to rehabilitate, evaluate, and then re-home the horses who come into the program. As the horses move into adoptive homes, you'll be able to bring more into the program. Additionally, adoption fees can help offset some costs of rehabilitation.

The drawbacks to an adoption program are the need to develop an effective screening process for adopters, the worry about where the horses will end up, and the need to promote your adoption program in order to find homes for the horses.

How Will You House the Horses?

If you opt for an adoption program, you'll have several additional decisions to make. Will you house the horses in a central rescue-intake facility, or will you work through a network of foster homes? This may depend on what facilities and resources you already have available. Rescues with their own facilities have an advantage in that they have a location to hold fund-raisers, work days, and open houses. Donors can drop off horses and other items at the facility, and adopters can look at several horses in one place.

Some organizations with central facilities also operate foster-home networks. In this case, the central facility then becomes an intake station, or a place where horses with behavioral problems can be held until they're deemed safe for placement in a foster home.

If you don't have access to a property where you can set up your facility, developing a network of foster homes will still enable you to help many horses. In fact, this arrangement allows horses to get more individual attention and can diffuse the workload. Some programs with foster-home networks require the temporary caretakers to pay some of the horses' bills, which helps the organization with the costs of rehabilitation. This type of program also allows rescues to bring in more horses than they might have space or funds to support at a single facility. Another advantage is that you may find foster homes with training or marketing experience, which can help make your horses easier to place.

However, foster-home networks have drawbacks, too. You'll need to develop a screening program to make sure that your foster homes can adequately provide for your horses. You also may need to implement an ongoing site-inspection program to ensure that the foster homes continue to provide proper care. Additionally, you'll have to be ready and able to quickly move horses out of foster homes when they're not working out.

How Will Your Rescue Support Itself?

How much money you'll need to support the rescue depends on how your organization is set up and the number of horses you plan to help. If you run a sanctuary where they remain for life, you'll have to bring in enough income to support those horses, many of whom will develop medical problems as they age.

If you run a facility where the horses are adopted out, you'll need funds to support the horses while they're at your facility, including money to treat illnesses, injuries, and malnutrition. Both sanctuaries and rescue facilities need to raise money for repairs and maintenance. And at some point, your organization may become big enough that it'll need money to pay full-time employees.

Depending on how it's set up, a rescue with a foster network may not need to raise as much money as one with its own facility. However, while it won't have a facility to maintain or repair, it'll still have to pay for hauling horses to foster homes, and for the cost of screening and checking up on those homes. Regardless of the type of organization you choose to set up, you'll find that fund-raising is critical.

Do You Want Members?

Some rescues set up membership programs to help bring in some of the income necessary to run the organization, while others recruit members to assist with running the rescue. Along with generating income, however, members also generate more work. You'll need to provide your members with some kind of benefit, such as a newsletter about the organization's horses, upcoming fund-raisers, clinics, etc., or the ability to adopt a horse before it becomes available to the general public.

You'll also need to consider whether or not you want to give the members a right to vote. In many rescues, the members are nonvoting—that is, they don't vote on the rescue's policies or mission, or for the directors or officers. Other rescues offer limited voting rights to their members, such as the ability to elect directors or a membership representative who sits on the board of directors.

Determine the Scope of Your Rescue

When you set up your organization, consider what types of horses you want to work with. Some organizations concentrate on rescuing horses from one specific source, such as auctions or feedlots, while others focus on many different sources. Some focus on a particular breed or a particular type of horses (e.g., Miniature Horses or racehorses); others accept only horses that are donated when their owners can no longer care for them. (Sometimes these are healthy horses that are easy to place into an adoption program, but often, donated horses have health or lameness problems.)

There are also organizations that focus on investigating cases of equine neglect and abuse, working with law enforcement to get the animals seized, preparing court cases, and then rehabilitating and re-homing the animals. Many rescues, such as Bluebonnet, don't limit themselves at all and will help any horse that's in need.

Don't Put the Cart Before the Horse

Now that you have a clear definition of your rescue and its scope, you're ready to start getting it officially organized. At this point, it's tempting to jump into rescue work without taking this next step, or without getting the proper paperwork in place (covered in Chapter 4). However, doing so can impair your ability to do rescue work over the long-term—a lesson I learned from personal experience.

Case in point: Valerie O'Brien, of Fableview Equine Rescue in Missouri, says her organization was still compiling the necessary paperwork for nonprofit status when it became clear there was an overwhelming need for rescue in Missouri. They quickly went from receiving a request for assistance every two to three months to receiving several requests each month.

An increasing workload such as this can be hard to handle without procedures and policies in place. And because the need for rescue grows every year, it's important that you consider your rescue's organizational set-up, get your legal paperwork together, and format your policies before you jump into rescue work. Furthermore, potential donors, adopters, and volunteers are going to ask questions about your organization's structure and policies before they're willing to get involved or make donations.

When I set up Lone Star with the aid of several charter members, we discussed all the particulars of our organization, then we dove into saving horses—before all of our paperwork and policies were in place. As a result, we were spread thin because we had to care for and find permanent homes for the horses already in our program, promote the rescue, and finish our paperwork and policies, all at the same time. If we'd gotten all the official business taken care of first, before jumping in and saving horses, we would have been much better organized in our first year of operation. Consequently, when I began forming Bluebonnet I'd learned from past mistakes and put our structure and paperwork in place before we took in any horses.

Develop A Mission Statement

A mission statement is a brief (one to three sentences) description of the goals, or mission, for your organization. It sets the tone for how your rescue will operate and gives potential board members, officers, volunteers, and donors an overview of your rescue organization's philosophy. It'll often be the first thing potential donors or volunteers will read about your organization, and if properly done, can tell them a great deal about your rescue.

Your mission statement should limit the scope of your organization so you won't go off in too many directions at once, and give direction and encouragement to volunteers. As you grow, it's helpful to review your mission statement from time to time to see if you're still on track.

Assemble a BOD

The BOD, or board of directors, is a group of people who will guide your organization. They'll design and review the policies the organization will follow. Day-to-day decisions may be left to the officers or the staff (volunteer or paid), but the BOD ultimately controls the organization's direction. In addition to developing policies, they'll appoint key volunteer positions, hire paid employees, and approve changes to the bylaws and articles of incorporation.

A logical question at this point is how many people do you need to have on the BOD? In the beginning, it's better to have a small board, and five to seven members seems to work well. Too often, young rescues put too many people on their BOD, and find it difficult to reach decisions.

Some organizations use a board position as a reward for someone who has put in many volunteer hours or donated a large sum of money. Others fill their BOD with family and friends. However, because the job of the directors is so important, you need to be careful when filling these positions. While you want people who agree with your mission statement and the organization's structure, you also want people with unique experience and expertise that'll help your organization grow and develop, while furthering your goals.

For instance, having a veterinarian and/or a farrier as well as a professional horse trainer on your BOD can help you write veterinary procedures and decide how much to budget for training expenses. Having a director with human-resource experience can help you handle problems between volunteers, donors, or adopters. Someone with financial experience can help with accounting and/or fund-raising, and an attorney can help you through legal issues.

When you've identified potential directors, schedule an individual meeting with each one to discuss your plans for the rescue. Tell each candidate what prompted you to start your organization and describe its proposed structure. Bring a copy of your mission statement and any other paperwork you may have put together. Explain the qualifications you believe they'd bring to the board to help make it strong, and ask for their ideas and input. At the end of your meeting, if you feel the candidate would be a valuable addition, ask them to consider joining the BOD.

In addition to a BOD, you might want to appoint an advisory board to provide advice and support. This group doesn't vote on policies, procedures, or other issues, but instead makes recommendations to the BOD. The board, in turn, may assign the advisory board an issue to examine and research.

Your advisory board might consist of horse trainers, veterinarians, farriers, and others who are involved in the horse industry. Their role could include devising plans to help your organization work with other professional organizations, market your adoptable horses, or raise funds. The advisory board can also tackle problems your BOD doesn't have time to research, and their recommendations can help the BOD make decisions regarding new projects, policies, and programs.

Select Officers

You have the option of electing officers from within your board of directors or from a separate pool of people. When your BOD and officers are separate, you can better define the jobs of director and officer, and will gain the benefit of different perspectives on the organization, how it's running, and what needs to be improved. At the same time, it can be difficult for a separate group of officers to enforce policies and goals they have no say in making. In Bluebonnet, our officers make up the executive committee of the BOD, so they have a say in the policies that govern the rescue.

In general, the directors guide the organization and make and revise its policies and procedures. Officers are generally responsible for the day-to-day operations of the organization and decision-making. The BOD is usually responsible for setting up the positions for officers and selecting individuals to fill them. It's important to keep in mind that as with a too-large BOD, too many officers can also lead to difficulty in decision-making. So in the beginning, it's best to keep the number of officer positions low—you'll need a president, secretary, and treasurer, while the position of vice president is optional.

With your structure in place, it's time to begin the paperwork that'll make your organization a reality. While a private rescue will require less paperwork than one that's nonprofit, a well-run organization with written policies available to the public will always be perceived as a more legitimate organization. So even if your rescue will be private, consider putting at least some of your structure into written policies. If you've chosen to set up your rescue as a 501(c)(3) organization, you'll need to complete paperwork with the state in which you plan to operate, as well as with the IRS.

SUMMARY OF POINTS TO CONSIDER WHEN YOU BEGIN TO SET UP YOUR RESCUE:

- ❏ **Create a long-range vision for the organization.**
- ❏ **Decide whether to run a private or nonprofit (public) rescue.**
- ❏ **Determine whether your organization will be run as a sanctuary or a rescue with an adoption program.**
- ❏ **Decide if you'll operate from a central rescue facility or will utilize a foster-home network.**
- ❏ **Identify what kind of financial support your organization will require.**
- ❏ **Decide whether your rescue will offer membership.**
- ❏ **Determine what type(s) of equines and/or circumstances will be the focus of your rescue.**
- ❏ **Create a mission statement.**
- ❏ **Assemble a board of directors.**
- ❏ **Select officers.**

Demeter and Persephone

Persephone was just one day old when she and her dam were removed from their negligent owner. Persephone's dam, Demeter, was several hundred pounds underweight and couldn't produce colostrum or enough milk. We worried that if we didn't get them out of their present circumstances they'd both die.

Demeter and Persephone stayed with a veterinarian for two weeks. He administered IV antibodies to Persephone to maintain her health, and gave Demeter plenty of nutritious food and fresh water. As a result, Demeter began producing healthy milk for her filly.

A few months after being removed from their negligent home, both Demeter and Persephone were healthy and fat, and little Persephone was growing. The saddest part of this story is that Demeter was once owned by

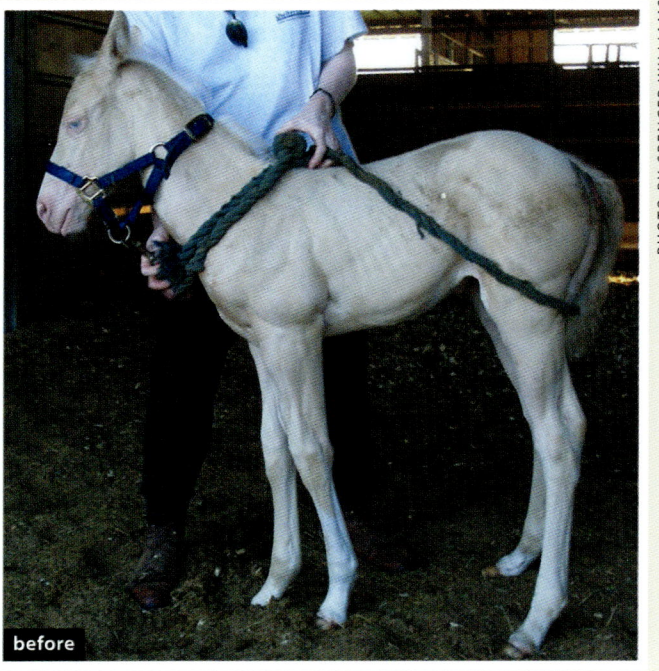

PHOTO BY SPENCER WILLIAMS

before

a woman who dearly loved and cared for her. She was a person who researched bloodlines, bought quality horses, and then bred them to produce horses with good conformation and great personalities.

But Demeter and Persephone's loving owner died, and her family didn't cherish her horses as she had. After a while, they stopped feeding them and the horses slowly lost weight. Sheriff's deputies visited the property and warned the family what would happen if the horses' care didn't improve, but they refused to listen. Everyone who knew the woman that had loved these horses knew that she'd be devastated if she saw their pitiful condition.

Fortunately, rescues exist to help horses exactly like these two. Since then, both Demeter and Persephone were adopted by loving families, and neither one will experience hard times again.

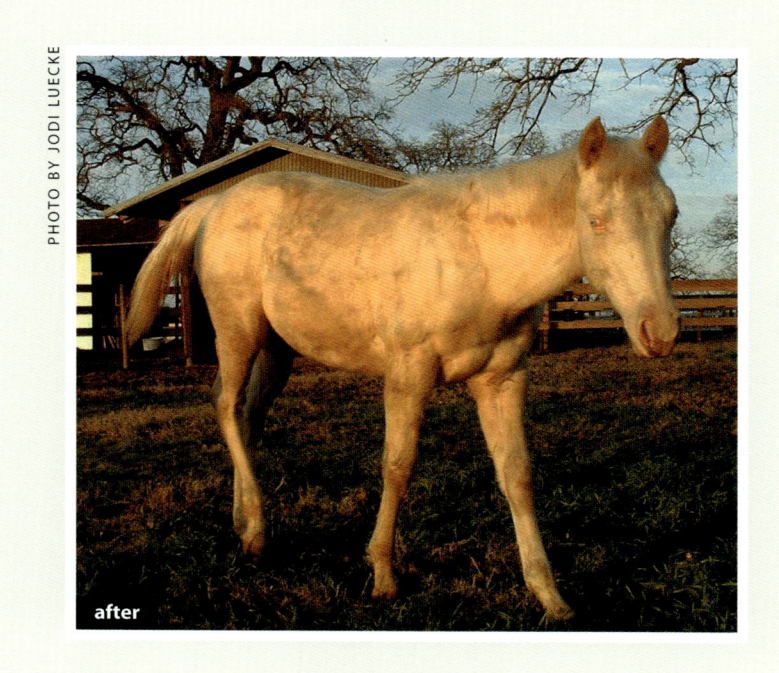

PHOTO BY JODI LUECKE

after

four

Prepare Your Paperwork

Although this step is undoubtedly tedious, you're almost there.

Pat yourself on the back. At this point, you've developed the framework for your rescue, organized a BOD, and may have selected a panel of officers. Now you're ready for the biggest, and most tedious, step of all—preparing the necessary paperwork. I'm going to assume you've chosen to become a legal, nonprofit corporation, because that's the most common decision. (If you've opted for a private rescue, refer to "The Pros and Cons of Private Rescue," on page 44.)

Although you may choose not to incorporate, first consider the following benefits of doing so:

- Incorporation creates a legal entity that can enter into contracts, incur debt, and pay taxes.
- Incorporation protects each of your board members and officers from being held personally liable in the event of a lawsuit, or for bills that may be incurred by the organization.

4 | *Prepare Your Paperwork*

> ## The Pros and Cons of Private Rescue
> For those of you who have decided to opt for private rescue, there are some advantages and some disadvantages. Consider the following:
> - **PRO:** You won't have to file articles of incorporation, write bylaws, or file paperwork with the IRS.
> - **CON:** Your state may consider your rescue work a business. If so, you'll be required to report as income all contributions, monies from fund-raisers, and adoption fees. While you may be thinking "everyone knows you can't actually make a profit doing rescue," the government only sees it one way—as income.
> - **PRO:** You may be able to write off expenses, such as hay, grain, the cost of buying horses at auction, and other costs of doing rescue. However, this requires detailed accounting.
>
> If you choose the private route, it might be wise to talk to an accountant for help filing proper tax forms.

- Incorporation will protect your organization's name and identity, because no two corporations can use the same name.
- Corporations often have more success in seeking grants.
- Corporations must operate under a formal set of rules, which lends credibility in the eyes of potential donors.
- A nonprofit corporation can earn a profit, but that profit must be reinvested in the organization (i.e., to pay employees, purchase equipment or facilities, expand programs and services, etc.). It cannot be given to members or directors as dividends.

You also have the option of whether or not to use an attorney to file paperwork for incorporation in your state and for tax-exempt status with the IRS. While some people will tell you not to attempt this step without legal assistance, many rescuers have successfully done so. In fact, I completed the paperwork for both Lone Star and Bluebonnet on my own. It took me more time than it may have taken an attorney, and it required great attention to detail, but it saved the fledgling organizations a good deal of money.

I'm going to assume you've decided to incorporate. Here's what you'll need to do to move forward....

Choose a Name

When you've reached a decision, call the secretary of state in your area to determine if the name you've chosen is available—meaning it's not being used by any other corporation. If it's available, you can normally reserve a name for a fee, which will then allow you a certain amount of time (60 to 120 days) to get the paperwork together to form a legal corporation using that name.

Apply for an Employee Identification Number (EIN)

Even if your organization won't have any paid employees, you still need to apply to the IRS for an EIN. This number identifies your organization with the IRS, and is the number that you'll give to donors so they can receive a tax deduction. This is also the number that'll be used when applying for tax-exempt status and filing annual reports with the IRS. You may file for an EIN online, through the mail, or via fax. You'll need the following information to apply for an EIN:

- The name, street, and mailing address of your organization.
- The name of the principal officer (the person who will be responsible for official paperwork or communication from the state and IRS).
- Type of entity—corporation (if you'll be filing paperwork to become a nonprofit, you'll be doing so as a corporation); sole proprietorship (an unincorporated rescue run solely by you—in other words a private rescue); partnership; or trust.
- Reason for applying—for example, you started a new business (rescue);

acquired an existing business (rescue) without an EIN; or changed the type of organization, such as from private to nonprofit.
- Number of employees your organization plans to have in the next 12 months.
- Purpose of the organization.
- Description of any merchandise that will be sold.

Develop Articles of Incorporation

Your next task is to write your Articles of Incorporation (these are also referred to as Articles of Association or a Constitution) and file them with your state. Exact requirements will vary from state to state, but your secretary of state can provide a list of guidelines and fees for filing Articles of Incorporation. Most states now offer this information online at their secretary of state's homepage. For most states, your Articles of Incorporation need to include:

- The name of your organization
- Name of principal officer
- Address of principal office
- Statement of purpose/mission statement
- List of founding directors
- Statement that defines what will happen to the corporation's assets if it's disbanded.

Write Bylaws

After you've sent your Articles of Incorporation to the appropriate state agency, you can begin writing your bylaws. The purpose of your bylaws is to describe how your organization will be run, who will be involved, and the intended purpose. Your bylaws should be easy to read and understand, and should answer procedural questions without being too detailed. You'll need to include the following sections:

- **Description of the organization.** In addition to specifying the legal name of your organization, this section provides basic information about it. It should include a description of purpose, which may be the same as your mission statement. This section also specifies the duration of your organization; in the case of most rescue organizations, you'll be establishing a "perpetual" organization (as opposed to a corporation that's formed for a specific length of time in order to put on a single event, such as a dog walk, to benefit multiple rescues). You also need to designate a principal office in this section, and should define your fiscal year. *Note:* While it may be tempting to set your fiscal year from January 1 to December 31, take into consideration that annual reports will be due soon after the end of your fiscal year. In this case, that means immediately following the busy holiday season, and right before personal tax returns are due. With this in mind, you may want to make the end of your fiscal year in the summer or fall.
- **Membership information.** This section defines whether or not your organization will have members. If you will, it should describe your members, including required qualifications (if any), their rights (e.g., voting) and responsibilities, terms of membership, and the procedure for termination. Some organizations allow members to transfer their memberships to others. If you don't want to allow this, it needs to be clearly stated in this section.
- **Meetings.** These include an annual meeting, general membership meetings, meetings of the officers and BOD, and special meetings. Be sure to include:
    - When each scheduled meeting will be held
    - The purpose of each meeting
    - How notice of the meetings will be distributed
    - How topics can be submitted for the meeting agenda
    - The necessary "quorum" (minimum number of members required) for decision-making.

This section should also address the procedure for calling a special meeting, and circumstances that might make this necessary.

- **Board of directors and officers.** Your bylaws will also need sections describing the board of directors and officers. These two sections will be similar, and both should include:
  - A description of the powers/responsibilities of individuals serving as officers or directors
  - Necessary qualifications
  - Nomination process
  - Term of office
  - Election procedure
  - Compensation
  - Procedures for removing an officer or director
  - Description of how vacancies are filled.
- **Committees, amendments, and dissolution.** These sections are simpler than some of those mentioned above. The section on committees describes how they're formed, who can be on a committee, and their scope of power. Some possible committees are: adoption, fund-raising, and nominating (to nominate officers and/or directors).

The procedure for making amendments to the bylaws should be outlined in its own section. It should include information on who can propose amendments, the process by which they are considered (e.g., does the BOD discuss them at a meeting, or are the members required to discuss them), and who votes on proposed amendments.

The dissolution section describes the procedure for shutting down the organization, and what will be done with its assets. Generally, a nonprofit organization is dissolved by a vote of either the BOD, officers, or members (as defined in the bylaws), and the organization must give its assets (horses, money, and any property) to another 501(c)(3) organization. *Note:* The assets of the organization cannot be given to individuals.

Apply for Nonprofit Status

With your bylaws written, you're almost done. The next step is to apply to the IRS for tax-exempt status. You'll need to get Publication 557, Tax-Exempt Status for Your Organization, which you can pick up at a local IRS office or download at www.irs.gov/. This publication discusses the rules for organizations seeking tax exemption under Section 501(a) of the Internal Revenue Code, and how to apply for this status. You'll need to file Form 1023, Application for Recognition of Exemption Under Section 501(c)(3) of the Internal Revenue Code. All applications must be complete and accompanied by a filing fee.

Along with the appropriate forms, when you apply for tax-exempt status you must also provide the IRS with your EIN number (see page 45); a copy of your Articles of Incorporation (see page 46) and the Certificate of Incorporation (if available), and any other organizational documents you've compiled. You should also include a copy of your bylaws.

All attachments to your application should be labeled with the organization's name, address, and EIN. Your application will need to include a description of your organization's purpose and activities, as well as financial statements from the current year and previous three years, or a proposed budget for two full years if your organization is not yet in operation.

After you've submitted your paperwork to the IRS, you'll have to wait to receive notification of your status. Sometimes this process can take up to six months or more. If you're approved, but your organization is not yet in operation, or has been in operation for less than five years, you'll receive a predetermination letter that grants provisional tax-exempt status for the first five years of operation. After the first five years, your status will be reviewed and the provisional status may be removed. If the IRS has questions or concerns about your application, it may contact you and give you a chance to work out any problems. (*Note:* If you're approved and you've already been in operation for at least five years, you'll receive a determination letter from the IRS granting you tax-exempt status.)

Upon receipt of your IRS Determination letter, your rescue must continue to meet certain requirements to maintain your 501(c)(3) status. Copies of your annual reports and application for exemption must be available to the public. If you receive a request for copies of these documents, you can mail them out within a reasonable period of time, make them available at a reasonable place of your choosing, or maintain them on your Web site. If, however, you have an office, then these documents must always be available during office hours.

Additionally, for any year in which your organization grosses over $25,000, you'll have to file an annual report. And if your organization has engaged in trade or business that's not substantially related to the charitable purposes of your organization, you may be required to pay income tax on the funds generated from these activities. For instance, monies earned from using rescue horses in a lesson program, boarding nonrescue horses, and training nonrescue horses are all examples of business income that's not related to your organization's charitable purpose (which is to rescue horses from potentially dangerous situations, according to your organization's definition of such situations). You may want to contact the IRS or hire an accountant if you have any question about whether or not certain income is taxable.

You're Almost There

Now you have up to six months to kill, right? Well, not quite. While you're waiting for the determination letter from the IRS, use this time to work on policies and procedures, applications, contracts, and standard operating protocols (SOPs). Remember, once you have all this official paperwork behind you, you'll never have to do it again—and the better defined your organization is now, the less questions and confusion there'll be later on. So let's get started…

- **Policies and procedures.** These are the written rules of your organization. A policy is a plan of action for dealing with a specific event; the procedures are the specific series of steps to be followed in order to accomplish that plan of action. As such, volunteers, donors, and adopters alike have something to which they can refer to learn exactly what to expect from your organization in any given situation, as well as what is expected from them. Your policies should always be available to anyone who requests them. All of the Bluebonnet policies have been placed on our Web site where anyone can download them. We'll also mail copies to people who don't have Internet access.

The policies of an organization are generally written and approved by the BOD. However, a good board will seek input from rescue members and officers, as well as from such experts as veterinarians, trainers, etc., when developing or revising policies.

You'll need a policy for each major process within your rescue. (Refer to "Examples of Rescue Policies," on page 52.) You need to put a lot of thought into writing these policies because they define how your organization will conduct its business. Again, consider the organization's mission statement, the type of rescue you plan to run, and your goals.

For example, since I wanted Bluebonnet to operate as a network of foster homes capable of rehabilitating horses for adoption, I knew I needed to write both a fostering policy and an adoption policy. I first outlined what the policy should contain: how Bluebonnet would conduct adoptions, and the required steps to determine a prospective adopter's eligibility; how adopters would be approved; and their obligations to Bluebonnet.

Additionally, we needed a policy detailing the criteria for putting a horse up for adoption, and how each one's adoption fee would be determined. Once I had completed this outline, I began to flesh out each section of the policy. The rescue's officers, directors, and members discussed how we would determine when a horse was eligible to go up for adoption, and decided he/she

4 | *Prepare Your Paperwork*

would need to be at a healthy weight, have been vaccinated for rabies, flu/rhino, and VEWT (Venezuelan/eastern/western encephalitis and tetanus), and be on a regular deworming and hoof-care schedule.

We discussed the steps for eligibility to adopt, and decided to require an application, three reference letters, and a pre-adoption home visit. We also opted to prohibit our adopters from breeding or reselling any horse they adopted from us, and included that information in our policy. Additionally, to

Examples of Rescue Policies

To develop policies, you first need to identify the major activities in which your rescue organization will be engaged, then write a policy for each. Based on Bluebonnet's list of policies, here are some suggestions:

- **Abuse/neglect investigation policy:** Explain how your organization will take a report of abuse/neglect; a step-by-step description of how it will conduct an investigation; and what you'll do with the information you gather.
- **Adoption policy:** Include who'll have the authority to determine when a horse is ready to be put up for adoption; how you'll arrive at an adoption fee; what will be required of prospective adopters; and what their expectations may be.
- **Disclosure policy:** Describe exactly what type of information about the horses will be disclosed to potential adopters.
- **Equine donation policy:** Describe the steps that must be followed to donate a horse. This should include the types of equines the rescue can not/will not accept; whether or not the rescue will accept horses without current, negative Coggins tests; and whether or not the rescue will charge a donation fee. If your rescue will require the donor to deliver his horse, or provide certain paperwork, include that information in this policy, too.
- **Emergency evacuation policy:** Explain how horses will be evacuated from the rescue facility should there be a natural disaster or emergency.
- **Euthanasia policy:** Define how the rescue will decide when it's necessary to euthanize a horse. For example, Bluebonnet officers vote on euthanasia. The exception to this would be a horse that's in great pain/distress, when a decision must be made immediately. In that case, if the attending veterinarian recommends euthanasia, the foster home or a solitary officer can authorize it.
- **Fostering policy:** Explain eligibility requirements to become a foster home; the application process; and what expenses the foster home will be responsible for.

ensure that each horse would be safe in his new adoptive home, we agreed we would conduct follow-up visits. And this information, too, was included in our adoption policy. (See Appendix I, on page 246.)

Bluebonnet also has additional policies that are specific to programs our organization offers, and if your rescue offers unique programs, you'll need to write additional policies to describe them as well. Keep in mind that policy development is a continual process. As your rescue grows, you'll develop new

- **Inspection policy:** Explain when inspections of foster and adoptive homes are conducted; who will conduct them; and how they'll be done.
- **Inspector policy:** Explain who's eligible to become an inspector for the rescue; the application process; what's expected of an inspector; and what training is available and/or required.
- **Legislation policy:** Explain whether or not the organization will be involved in lobbying to influence legislation.
- **Membership policy:** Describe membership-eligibility requirements; how to become a member; and the cost of membership.
- **Money donation policy:** Explain whether or not donations are tax-deductible; the paperwork that must accompany donations; and the terms under which the organization will issue a receipt.
- **Policy development policy:** Describe how policies are developed and revised, and how to suggest policy revisions.
- **Reimbursement policy:** Explain the necessary steps to obtain reimbursement for expenses associated with volunteer work.
- **Transportation policy:** Explain the process used to transport horses, and be sure to cover such issues as insurance, who will be authorized to transport horses, and any paperwork that must be completed prior to transport.
- **Transportation volunteer policy:** Describe necessary qualifications to transport horses on behalf of the rescue, including any application process or any other paperwork that must be on file for eligibility.
- **Veterinary procedures policy:** Explain how the organization will arrive at a decision to seek veterinary care. (*Note:* At Bluebonnet, the Veterinary Procedures Policy requires a foster home to get prior approval for veterinary treatment, with exceptions made in life-threatening circumstances as long as the costs don't exceed $650. For veterinary treatments that cost under $250, a single officer may approve the expense; for treatments over $250, the majority of the officers must agree. The Veterinary Procedures Policy for Bluebonnet also outlines how a veterinary bill can be handled—either directly through the organization, or through the foster home, which can then submit a request for reimbursement.)

programs, and will need new policies to determine how they'll be run. You'll also refine your original policies as you learn from your experiences. It's a good idea to review your policies annually to determine if you need to update or revise them.

- **Applications and Contracts.** As your policies develop, so will your need for applications and contracts to go along with them. These may need to be revised as your rescue grows and you learn more, so it's a good idea to review applications and contracts at the same time you do your annual policy review.
- **Standard Operating Protocols (SOPs).** These describe step-by-step procedures for handling specific tasks, in greater detail than found in the policies and procedures. For instance, your membership policy may state that the membership coordinator will receive and process applications, and renewals will be sent by e-mail and postal mail one month prior to membership expiration. The protocol for membership processing might further define the policy as follows:
  - Membership coordinator receives applications and enters all information in membership database.
  - Membership coordinator sends new members their Member Introduction Packet.
  - Membership coordinator invites new members to the e-mail list.
  - Assistant membership coordinator calls new members to welcome them to the rescue and ask if they have any questions or need help getting more involved.

(*Note:* For a copy of Bluebonnet's Membership Application Processing SOP, see Appendix 2, on page 249.)

You'll need to develop an individual SOP for each routine task your organization will perform—unless your policies provide specific step-by-step details. In that case, you won't need SOPs. Just remember, the purpose is to provide volunteers with a place to look for crystal-clear directions on how every task should be handled.

After reading this chapter, you may think the amount of mental energy and paperwork you need to start a rescue organization is overwhelming. I promise you can make it through the paperwork, though, and the good news is that once it's done, you'll be ready to start rescuing horses!

SUMMARY OF NECESSARY PAPERWORK TO LAUNCH YOUR RESCUE:

- ❏ **Name reservation form**: to reserve your corporation's name; submit to the secretary of state in your state.
- ❏ **EIN form**: to identify your organization to the IRS; also used when issuing receipts for tax-deductible donations; submit to the IRS.
- ❏ **Articles of Incorporation**: to facilitate your organization becoming a legal corporation; submit to the secretary of state for your state.
- ❏ **Bylaws**—to describe how your organization will be run and who will be involved; necessary when applying for nonprofit/tax-exempt status; submit to the IRS.
- ❏ **Form 1023**: Application for Recognition of Exemption Under Section 501(c)(3) of the Internal Revenue Code: to become a nonprofit/tax-exempt corporation; submit to the IRS.
- ❏ **Policies and Procedures**: rules by which the organization will operate, and step-by-step guidelines on how to carry them out.
- ❏ **Applications and Contracts**: forms necessary to support policies and procedures and facilitate operation.
- ❏ **Standard Operating Protocols (SOPs)**: to outline how various routine tasks will be handled, and who will be responsible for each.

Gypsy

When Gypsy was seized from her negligent owners by law enforcement, they didn't even know she existed. Apparently, it had been well over a year since they last visited their horses, and Gypsy's dam hadn't appeared to be pregnant. So when Gypsy arrived at my barn at about 11 months of age, she'd been running free all of her short life. She had only been touched by a human once—when she was captured in a squeeze-chute and a veterinarian drew blood to run a Coggins test. I had my work cut out for me.

Gypsy spent her first several months in a large foaling stall. It gave her plenty of room to move around, and she saw humans walking by her stall several times each day. Initially, she plastered herself to the back of the stall whenever someone walked by. I knew she had to accept humans if she was ever going to be adopted, so every evening I put her feed in a bucket on the floor and I sat in the corner of her stall, reading a book and talking to her. At first she would only eat if the bucket was at least 10 feet away from me. Over the next several weeks I gradually moved the bucket closer and closer until she was comfortably eating within arm's length.

After we were able to catch and halter her, we began touching her, scratching her itchy spots, and teaching her to lead. She then moved into another foster home that taught her to stand tied, accept grooming and bathing, and to load into a trailer. Less than a year after she arrived at the rescue, Gypsy was as tame as any horse that had been handled from birth. She was adopted by a family who fell in love with her, and couldn't believe that Gypsy was once a Wild Child.

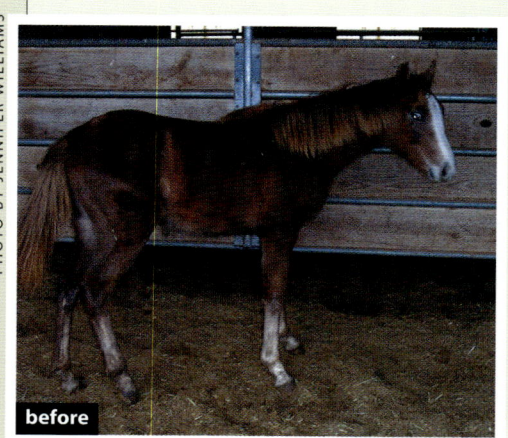

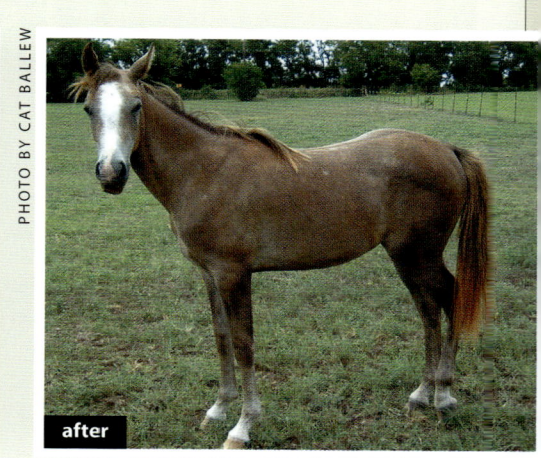

PHOTO BY JENNIFER WILLIAMS

before

PHOTO BY CAT BALLEW

after

five

Recruitment and Retention of Volunteers

Every volunteer is a valuable asset!

You've put in a lot of effort to get to this point—you've gotten your organizational structure in place and sent all your paperwork to the state and IRS. You're now ready to begin promoting your rescue, taking in horses, and placing them in adoptive homes. To accomplish this, you'll need a team of great volunteers to help you. While the specific volunteer needs of your rescue depend on how you set it up, the recruitment, training, and retention of volunteers are similar within all organizations.

My rescue, Bluebonnet, is entirely volunteer-run. Our volunteers are responsible for fostering horses, transporting them to their new homes, conducting pre-adoption and pre-fostering home visits, investigating reports of abuse and neglect, assisting law enforcement when seizing neglected equines, promoting the rescue, writing grants, and running the rescue's fundraisers. Bluebonnet couldn't operate without a strong volunteer base to accomplish all of these tasks, and more.

5 | Recruitment and Retention of Volunteers

Sometimes it may seem that volunteers are more work than they're worth. However, you'll quickly learn that every volunteer is a valuable asset! Some people will come to your organization ready to work; they'll be creative, full of ideas, and happy to jump right in. Bluebonnet is lucky to have many such volunteers. Even though some of them know very little about horses, they bring other talents, such as unique experience in public relations or fund-raising, that help us grow and improve. And, they bring new energy to the rescue.

Other people may be interested in working, but may be uncertain about their role and what they can do. A good volunteer-mentoring program can team up experienced volunteers with the newcomers. The mentors coach the new volunteers until they understand the organization and what's expected of them. Often, once they feel confident in their role in the organization, these volunteers become some of the hardest-working, most dedicated volunteers you'll find.

Both of these volunteer types will likely make a long-term commitment to your group, and you'll be able to rely on them for help with your workload. But you'll also encounter those who view volunteering as a social venture— a time to chat with people and make new friends. They help keep your organization fun, and while they aren't really interested in doing any of the dirty work, you can put them to work organizing social functions and awards programs.

There will also be people who'll come to your organization to volunteer, then will help out once or twice, or even for a few weeks, before drifting away. Often they discover there's more to volunteering than they thought, sometimes they just want a chance to ride the organization's horses, or other commitments may simply have limited their availability. You may also get volunteers who have to perform a set number of hours for community service. Sometimes this is court-ordered community service, although many high schools, colleges, fraternities, sororities, and other groups are now requiring that their students, members, or employees perform community-service hours, so you may also get people volunteering to meet these requirements.

Keep in mind that any volunteer—even one who's around for only a limited time—can aid your rescue. Again, they may come up with new ideas for fund-raising or promotion, or offer new solutions to problems. When I worked for Lone Star, one of our new members proposed having a one-day fund-raiser with a silent and live auction, as well as hourly clinics and demonstrations by trainers, farriers, and veterinarians. This event grew into a large fund-raising festival that brought in a significant amount of money. New volunteers can also jump in and energize your rescue efforts, and their enthusiasm can inspire those volunteers who currently feel burnt out or tired.

Always take the time to listen to what your volunteers say about your organization. New people may view your policies and structures in a different way. Volunteers and their questions make you think about your organization's structure, policies, and operation, and you may find areas you can strengthen. Or, they may want you to make changes you're unable or unwilling to make. For example, new members often ask us to waive our adoption fee when a foster home adopts a horse placed in their care. However, our directors are unwilling to do so because they believe there are many volunteers—in addition to the foster homes—who invest time and money in the rescue. Therefore, it would be unfair to reward some and not others.

Another new volunteer reviewed the procedure we used when investigating reports of neglect and drafted an "investigation form" that we implemented. Looking at your organization through your volunteers' eyes will help you determine if you're staying on track.

Define Volunteer Jobs

In the beginning, you may have trouble using volunteers. Often, the founders of nonprofit rescues yearn for volunteers to help with the workload, but when they finally get some volunteers, they aren't sure how to use them. Most likely, this is partly because they've become used to doing most of the work themselves and don't know how to delegate responsibilities.

Other times, founders worry that if a job is turned over to a volunteer it may not get done correctly. I felt this way in the beginning, but since then, I've learned that in order to effectively run a large organization I need to recruit people for some jobs. I used to assign only small jobs, and constantly supervised the volunteers. In time, I was able to delegate bigger jobs to volunteers I trusted, and I've learned to more easily identify jobs that volunteers can perform. Part of my job has become overseeing those volunteers to insure that jobs get done properly, and to provide assistance to the volunteers.

Using volunteers takes some effort, but it'll pay off in the long run. To start with, make a list of all the jobs that currently need to be done. Identify which of these jobs must be done by an officer or staff member. These would be the jobs that require extensive training, such as neglect investigations, or jobs that involve access to confidential information, such as adoption records, information about seizures, etc. Then put together a list of jobs you would like to see done that currently aren't getting done. Look over the two lists and prioritize the jobs according to which jobs are most critical to your organization at this time.

Once you've assembled a list of potential volunteer jobs, and have decided which ones are most important, you need to write job descriptions. Each job description should include:

- A title for the position
- Job purpose
- Responsibilities
- Qualifications
- Necessary time commitments.

The job description should also include how the position fits into the organization's structure, including who the volunteer reports to, and whether anyone will be reporting to the person who holds this position. You'll also need to describe time commitments (e.g., daily/weekly commitments), when the job needs to be done (during working hours, in the evenings, etc.), and the long-term goals for the job. The last part of the job description should include the benefits to the volunteer. (I'll cover these in a minute.)

How to Recruit Volunteers

Once you have a clear picture of the positions you need to fill, you'll be ready to begin recruiting people to get the work done. There are several ways to go about this:

- Run ads in local newspapers
- Put up booths at fairs, carnivals, horse shows, horse expos, and other events
- Post notices and fliers in tack and feed stores, and veterinary offices
- Ask local newspapers, television and radio stations to do a story on your organization, stressing the needs for volunteer assistance
- Explain your volunteer needs to local groups, including 4-H, FFA, high-school and college agriculture groups, and horse clubs

> **Cindy Fanning, a Bluebonnet volunteer, described the benefits of volunteering by saying, "When little Nigel comes up to me in the field and lets me scratch his forehead, I know I've done something good in restoring his trust. When Sprite kicks at Nigel at feeding time, I know I've helped to restore her trust. When the skinny horses nicker to me in the morning, I know I'm in the process of restoring their trust. What do I want from all this? I want nothing more than what I've just described—a scratch, a kicking of heels, a nicker."**

- Place ads in school papers, church bulletins, and other newsletters describing your rescue and the need for volunteers
- Post fliers in community centers, schools, and similar areas
- Hand out flyers or pamphlets about your organization to people at horse shows.

When you're recruiting volunteers you'll need to provide some information about your organization's purpose, including why it's needed, and what role volunteers play in it. Find out what skills potential volunteers have to offer, as well as what training they'll need. List the benefits of volunteering (which may include assisting in a worthwhile cause, meeting other like-minded people, volunteer awards, etc.). Tell prospective volunteers what others have to say about their experience, and if possible, introduce them to volunteers who can tell them about your organization and the time they've spent there.

When you recruit volunteers, remember to focus on the rewards of volunteering. According to volunteers I've spoken to, the benefits include:

- Helping needy horses
- Getting a chance to ride and train a variety of horses
- Learning about rehabilitation, lameness, and diseases
- Meeting other people who care about horses
- Learning about the amazing ability of horses to love and trust even after being starved or abused
- Getting a chance to give back to horses after getting so much from them.

Ways to Train Volunteers

Once you have newly recruited volunteers, you may need to provide training. The amount and type of training will depend on the position and the volunteer's current level of experience relative to that position. All training should begin with an overview of your organization, including a brief history, your mission statement, your organization's current goals, and an overview of the group's current projects. (If you have access to a copy machine, you might even want to put all this together in a take-home packet.) Then you can focus on specific training for the tasks your volunteer(s) will be performing. Provide a description of the amount of time the job may take, and conclude with a list of the rewards of volunteering (refer to page 62).

Some organizations provide training to groups of volunteers in person. Others pair a new volunteer with an experienced person who can mentor them and teach them the ropes. You also can provide training online or use training manuals to provide instruction. Decide what will work best for your rescue and begin developing your volunteer-training program.

I'm currently developing online training for the Bluebonnet volunteers who'll investigate reports of abuse and neglect. Through computer technology, the rescue will host an online class that meets one night each week. During the class, I'll teach participants how to take a report of neglect or abuse, how to investigate these cases, and how to work with law-enforcement officers to conduct a seizure. The class will be offered several times a year to enable busy volunteers to fit it into their schedules.

How to Keep 'em Coming Back!

Just as important as getting volunteers is keeping them around. To some extent, this depends on how you train them, the environment in which they work, and how you treat them. When you provide good training and a well-defined task to perform, people are less likely to get frustrated or lose interest. If you provide a fun place in which to work, a chance to meet other people, and a supervisor who understands your volunteers' needs, everyone will perform better.

Even with the best programs, many volunteers will only show up a few

5 | Recruitment and Retention of Volunteers

times. Sometimes, the organization isn't what they're looking for, and other times they discover they really don't have enough time to continue working with your group. For every 10 casual helpers, you'll find one dedicated volunteer. While in the beginning you may restrict volunteers to noncritical jobs in your organization, over time you'll be able to give the few dedicated volunteers more responsibility.

The most difficult part of working with volunteers is keeping them coming back, and it takes time and planning. You'll need to make your volunteers feel they're an important part of your organization, and that they're appreciated. Here are some suggestions to help accomplish this:

- *Give volunteers some responsibility, and a well-defined position.* While you need them to give you status reports, don't require them to check in before and/or after everything they do.
- *Promote a friendly working environment.* Have get-togethers, group outings, or lunches to give volunteers a chance to socialize and meet new people.
- *Provide evaluations.* This will let your volunteers know how they're doing, and that you appreciate their contributions to the organization.
- *Incorporate volunteer awards, or other forms of volunteer recognition.* Large organizations sometimes put on elaborate galas or dinners where they present awards to their key volunteers, but small organizations may not have the finances to do so. However, there are still many ways to recognize your volunteers, such as…
  • Include a "Volunteer of the Month" column in your newsletter or post a list of important volunteers on your Web site.
  • Send your volunteers handwritten thank-you notes or certificates of appreciation.
  • If volunteers organize an event, thank them in the event's program. Throw a "volunteer appreciation" luncheon or cookout once a year.

People who believe they're making a difference are more likely to stick with an endeavor. So make sure you let your volunteers know just how valuable they are.

What to Do When Problems Arise

Unfortunately, sometimes volunteers don't work out, and rescuers often have difficulty dealing with these situations. New organizations fear turning away any volunteer, and might be tempted to let small things slide or to try especially hard to work with a problematic individual. Some rescue directors are reluctant to confront volunteers about poor behavior, and others just don't know how or what to say. Regardless, if you have a volunteer who isn't working out, you need to act.

Other than behavior, there are many ways in which a volunteer might not work out. These include a failure to complete tasks, poor performance on tasks, or not showing up for volunteer shifts. When a volunteer doesn't do her job, the organization suffers. You may have to pick up the slack and finish jobs so the rescue doesn't appear disorganized and unprofessional to outsiders, and this may leave other tasks unfinished.

Before you act, consider possible reasons for this person's actions. For instance, maybe the volunteer is performing poorly because she doesn't understand her job, doesn't like it, or isn't really interested in the organization. Then, schedule a time to talk to the volunteer. Explain that you appreciate her contributions to the organization, but you're concerned about how things are going and want to discuss how you can make them better. Explain why her volunteer job is important and how the organization suffers if the job isn't completed or isn't done well. When you discuss problems regarding her work, be sure to use specific examples and facts to back up your complaints. Don't bring up unverified rumors.

Next, ask the volunteer for her input—does she need more training, or

5 | Recruitment and Retention of Volunteers

would she prefer another job? After you've agreed on a solution, be sure to check up on how things are going. If the problems continue, you may need to tell the individual that while you appreciate her intentions, it doesn't appear that she's in the spot best-suited for her abilities. Offer her another volunteer job, perhaps one that's less critical to your organization, but also explain that you'll understand if she's too busy to continue volunteering and needs to give up her position. Sometimes people perform poorly or don't show up because they're too busy but are too shy to quit volunteering, or feel guilty about doing so.

Occasionally, you'll encounter more serious volunteer problems, such as an individual who becomes dissatisfied with your rescue or the way you run it. Instead of talking to you about her problems, she may decide to complain to other volunteers, prospective adopters, donors, or members of the rescue or community. In other cases, an individual may dislike you or other key volunteers, and gossip about them to other volunteers or people outside your organization. This is a touchy situation as such a person can damage your rescue's reputation and may even cause you to lose money and/or good homes for your horses, as well as affect your ability to get, or keep, other volunteers.

When you discover a disgruntled volunteer who's gossiping or spreading rumors about your organization, you need to act fast, but you also need to be prepared. First, talk to the people involved to learn more about what the individual has said or done. When you've spoken to several people who've heard the volunteer spreading rumors or have been affected by the volunteer's poor behavior, arrange a meeting with that person. Then explain the reason for the meeting and what you discovered while talking to people with whom she's interacted.

Finally, ask her what's wrong, and if there's any way you can help resolve her dissatisfaction with the organization. Explain that spreading rumors, gossiping, and similar behavior is absolutely unacceptable in your organization and give her a chance to make amends. However, if the behavior persists, this is one volunteer you can do without. Call her in for another meeting and explain that you feel this volunteer relationship isn't working out, and her presence is no longer a benefit to the organization. This is a hard situation to handle, but you need to handle it quickly if your rescue is to succeed.

Bottom line: Your organization needs volunteers to help carry some of the workload. And if it's to run smoothly, you must be prepared to spend money on your volunteer program. You'll need to set aside funds for recruitment, as well as the development of training and recognition/awards programs. In the end, though, good volunteers will enable your organization to expand its programs and develop a more professional attitude and appearance. While this may seem like a lot of work, it's a worthwhile investment in the long-term growth and health of your organization.

Serena

The sun beat down on Serena and her pasturemates as a deputy responded to the complaint of starving horses. The yearling half-Arabian filly was thin—but what was even more worrisome was the deputy couldn't find any water on the property. The tanks were dry and full of leaves, and there didn't appear to be running water anywhere.

The deputy called the rescue for help, and as we prepared to remove the animals, the sheriff ordered the local water company to truck in water for the thirsty horses. They crowded around for a drink as the water splashed into the empty tank. After the horses drank their fill, rescue volunteers began catching them and loading them into a horse trailer. They were headed to a local clinic where a veterinarian could check them over.

Luckily, none of the horses seemed to suffer any ill effects from dehydration, and they were all moved into foster homes that could begin rehabilitating them. As Serena gained weight, she also won the heart of her foster mom. It wasn't long before Cindy knew that she couldn't let Serena leave the farm, and Cindy adopted the filly.

Today Serena is healthy and happy, and her adoptive mom is teaching her (Pat) Parelli's Seven Games in preparation for the day when Serena is old enough to begin saddle training.

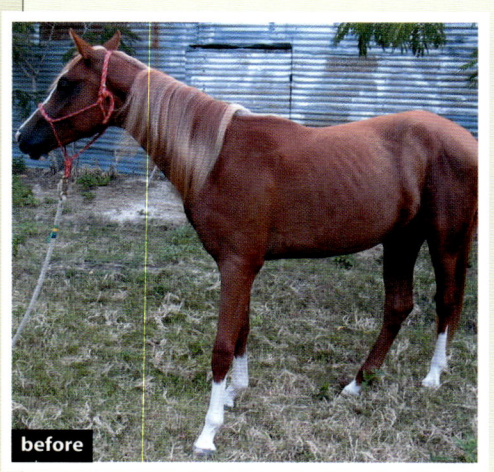

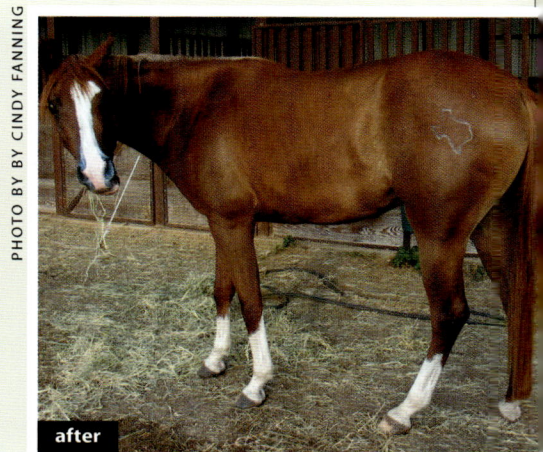

PHOTO BY BY CINDY FANNING — before

PHOTO BY BY CINDY FANNING — after

six

Public Relations

PR plays a crucial role in the success and longevity of your rescue efforts.

Many rescuers overlook the importance of public relations and fail to commit the necessary time and energy to develop a comprehensive PR program. However, aggressive PR is essential not only to promote your organization and its activities, but also to build and guard your reputation. The latter is especially important as it will attract new members, volunteers, and adopters, as well as ensure continuing support from donors—all of which will help your rescue grow and carry out its mission. PR can also provide a way to introduce your group and its efforts to law-enforcement officers and other rescue agencies.

Your PR coordinator's main role will be to maintain public awareness of your organization, with an emphasis on its integrity. As guardian of your rescue's image, this person should present a professional image to the public. Your PR coordinator will also be responsible for gathering feedback from the public, which can be used to help the rescue design and improve programs,

6 *Public Relations*

> **THE ROLE OF PR COORDINATOR**
>
> The job of a public relations coordinator is more complex than simply writing and distributing press releases about an organization's activities. She also may be responsible for the following:
>
> - Writing public-service announcements
> - Creating promotional material, including brochures and fliers
> - Preparing presentations for groups of potential volunteers or donors
> - Creating sponsorship packages
> - Researching and writing grants
> - Working with the media to generate television and/or newspaper coverage
> - Advertising to increase public awareness, draw in new volunteers, and reach potential adopters
> - Producing reports for both members and the public about the organization's activities and status
> - Assisting other staff members in planning events designed to raise awareness

policies, and that all-important public image. There are many ways to accomplish these goals, so we'll go through them one-by-one.

Press Releases

These are short (often one page) articles that describe a specific event or achievement. For instance, Bluebonnet uses press releases to promote fund-raising events, announce milestones achieved by the organization, and to release information on neglect cases.

Press releases should include the following information:

- *Title*: Keep it short, but provide pertinent information. (For an example, refer to the sample press release in Appendix 3, page 250; the title provides the organization's name, as well as the purpose and location of the event.

- ***What:*** Describe the event that will be taking place or the seizure that recently occurred.
- ***When and where:*** Include dates, times, and when appropriate, the location. (*Note:* An address isn't appropriate when releasing details of a seizure. Bluebonnet only provides the name of the city and/or county.)
- ***Why:*** Describe the purpose of an event (e.g., to raise funds for XYZ), and include a plea for donations or participants. Also, be sure to tell readers how they can obtain more information.
- ***Who:*** In the body of the press release, include the name of your organization and any other relevant organizations or individuals. (*Note:* Press releases describing seizures should not include the owners' names, especially if the case is still pending in court.)
- ***Contact information:*** Always provide the name of your PR coordinator, the address and phone number of the organization, along with the Web site and e-mail address at the end of each press release.

Finally, you need to distribute press releases to any/all media outlets in the area of your event or seizure, including newspapers, television news shows, and radio stations. Many will run your press release, and some may follow up with a more in-depth article or story.

Promotional Materials

These include brochures, flyers, and booklets or pamphlets that provide information about your organization and its programs. Because brochures or flyers are often how potential volunteers and adopters first learn about your organization, they need to be eye-catching and easy to read. They should provide general information about your rescue, as well as the specific programs you offer, and should include an address and phone number so those who are interested can seek more information.

You also need flyers to announce fund-raisers and other specific events. Bluebonnet even has a "Wish List" flyer that details specific items the rescue needs. You can ask volunteers to leave promotional materials at feed and tack stores they frequent, distribute them to local veterinary offices, and pass them out at horse shows and other animal events they attend. (*Note:* It's always a good idea to first ask whoever's in charge if they mind you doing so.) Tri-fold brochures (those that open into three sections) work especially well for these purposes. Also, consider hanging flyers on community bulletin boards.

Special Presentations

Part of the PR coordinator's job also involves preparing presentations to educate groups of potential volunteers or donors about your organization. You may be asked to speak to a group of potential volunteers, such as a 4-H club, high-school agriculture class, or a local horse club. Other times, you may be invited to speak to a potential donor or sponsor, such as a large corporation or local feed store.

Be sure to ask the person coordinating the meeting what equipment will be available. This can range from equipment that works with a computer to display PowerPoint presentations to a slide projector; sometimes the only equipment that's available is an overhead projector. (*Note:* You can have slides or transparencies made from a PowerPoint presentation for use with a slide or overhead projector.) If you won't have access to any equipment, you can use printed handouts.

Regardless of the type of equipment you have to work with, the presentations put together by the PR coordinator need to be eye-catching, easy to follow, and interesting. A poor presentation will bore your audience, but a good one will keep them listening and create enthusiasm. Often, a corporation, local store, or horse club sees several presentations each year from organizations that are seeking money or volunteers. A good presentation will impress your audience, and they'll remember your organization when they're ready to take action.

While working with rescues, I've given several such presentations. One time I spoke to a group of children and parents at a local 4-H club. During my brief talk, I told the kids how they can help by asking their parents to report neglected horses or by fostering horses with their parents' help and permission. This presentation was driven by the kids' questions and was done without any equipment. At the end of my talk, I handed out brochures with the rescue's contact information.

On another occasion I gave a presentation to a corporation that was considering supplying our organization with a year's worth of hay. I gave this presentation at the corporate headquarters and was able to use a PowerPoint presentation full of photographs of the horses their donation would help. And when giving talks at the conventions held by the American Quarter Horse Association and the American Horse Council, I used both a PowerPoint presentation and handed out brochures.

Each presentation is different based on the audience and time limit, so the PR coordinator should prepare sample outlines for presentations to different types of groups and for different purposes. She can also help design PowerPoint presentations or materials to give participants for specific events.

Media Coverage

Newspapers, magazines, radio, and television are invaluable tools for reaching large numbers of people. Your PR coordinator needs to work with the media to get coverage for your organization and to locate free or reduced-rate advertising for your events. For instance, some local television news shows will be happy to feature your rescue and help spread the word regarding your need for donations and foster homes.

6 | Public Relations

When seeking television spots for our rescue, a volunteer researched a local television station and contacted an anchor who often presented animal stories. The volunteer presented information on the rescue, emphasizing the need for donations, members, and volunteers. The anchor was excited to find a horse rescue in the area, and put together a crew to visit a foster home and interview the family. The spot aired on the evening newscast a few days later and the hits on our Web site doubled for several days afterwards. We gained new members and foster homes.

Sometimes, however, a media resource will want to wait until you take in starving horses, or are holding an event before they'll do a story. For example, after the rescue was awarded horses in a neglect case, we sent a press release to the local news media, emphasizing the need for immediate assistance. They contacted us the day they received it and arranged to visit one of the horses that evening. The story gave brief background information on the rescue, but featured the starving horse I was rehabilitating. After the story aired, the rescue got at least 30 phone calls from people who were interested in helping or adopting horses.

Radio stations occasionally will allow your PR coordinator or another volunteer to come on one of their shows to talk about your group and its needs. Many stations will also air public-service announcements (PSAs), free of charge, to publicize events for nonprofit groups. Many volunteers from our rescue have been interviewed on the radio about horse neglect and how listeners can make a difference.

Your PR coordinator should also contact local newspapers and horse magazines. Bluebonnet obtained free advertising in a local phone book, as well as Texas-wide magazines. Some newspapers and local magazines will accept articles from outside contributors, so your PR coordinator (or a talented volunteer) should write about the rescue and submit articles to those publications. Others will send a reporter out or will interview you and other members over the telephone.

Another way to secure good PR for your organization is to ask your supporters to write letters to the editors of local newspapers. A woman I had helped to adopt a horse from the rescue did just this, almost two years after adopting her horse. In her letter, she discussed the organization and described the wonderful riding horse and companion she had adopted. She encouraged other readers to adopt and provided contact information for the rescue. After publishing her letter, a writer for the newspaper contacted her for an interview. Both the letter to the editor and the longer piece gave the rescue some great publicity.

Press Kits

Your PR coordinator will need a press kit when he/she contacts the media. The purpose of a good press kit is to introduce your organization and generate interest in its activities. While this kit should help to make your organization memorable, it should also encourage those reading it to contact you for more information.

Before sending out a press kit, your PR coordinator should research the media outlet to determine which person is most likely to be interested in animal-related stories and issues. By sending your kit directly to such a person you'll avoid wasting your precious resources, and will help ensure that it doesn't end up at the bottom of a pile. When possible, tie a press release to current events to further generate interest. For example, if there's a large horse show or rodeo in town that's attracting media attention, present your press kit to show the "other side" of the horse world. Or, if law-enforcement officers have seized horses or other animals anywhere in your area, let the media know that your rescue is prepared to assist needy equines.

One of our members caught a local news show that featured an out-of-state horse rescue. She sent them a press kit with a letter informing them that we were serving horses in their county. Within a week, they also featured a story on our organization. We've also sent out press releases with information on pending legislation that could affect the rescue, such as the American Horse Slaughter Prevention Act.

Following is the basic information your press kit should include:
- Your organization's history, including information about when and why it was founded, the number and type of equines you've taken in and adopted out, and other milestones.
- Current information on your organization, including the number of equines currently in your care, a description of your membership, a list of current activities, and a description of planned future events.
- Short biographies on the rescue's officers and directors. These should include a description of each person's education, horse experience, and the qualities each brings to the rescue.
- A business card or contact-information sheet. Be sure to include the names of both the PR coordinator and the president, in addition to your telephone number and street address, your e-mail address, and Web site.
- Any press releases sent out in the past two months. These will illustrate your rescue's activities.
- Photographs, including before-and-after shots of rescued horses, as well as the "happy endings" in their adoptive homes. These will provide reporters with a very visual example of what your organization is doing.

Advertising

Another job for your PR coordinator is the coordination of advertising campaigns.

When arranging an advertising campaign for a specific event, such as a clinic or adopt-a-thon, your PR coordinator should approach horse-related publications, as well as newspapers and news shows in the area. For a generalized advertising campaign, such as a membership drive or solicitation for donations, your PR coordinator should not only include the horse-related publications, but also all news shows and newspapers serving the region or state in which your group operates. As mentioned, some television and radio stations will run free ads or announcements for nonprofit groups. And, horse publications and newspapers often will either donate a classified ad or run one for a reduced rate if your organization is 501(c)(3).

Occasionally, Bluebonnet runs a classified ad in newspapers throughout the state of Texas reading, "Horse rescue: horses available for adoption; donations needed." The short ads are cheap to run in papers that won't donate the space, and generally result in several phone calls. The ads help bring in new members, potential adopters, and donors.

Activity Reports

Your PR person will also need to help assemble reports on your organization's activities. Internal reports to members and volunteers not only inform them about changes in policies and upcoming events, but also help build and maintain trust in the group's leadership. At Bluebonnet, each staff member (this includes directors, officers, and committee heads) e-mails a monthly activity report to the membership. Additionally, the minutes of the board of directors meetings are posted to the membership. Our monthly newsletter also contains membership and financial reports.

Transparency—the accurate, timely disclosure of information—is an important concept in nonprofit management. Your PR coordinator can improve your organization's transparency by generating reports for your supporters and the general public. Corporate sponsors and donors need to know how your organization conducts business before they'll contribute to your cause, and sheriff's departments and other rescue groups need to understand how your rescue operates before they'll agree to work with you.

Bluebonnet generates several reports. We make this information available to the public on our Web site, and also send copies to potential supporters upon request. **These reports include:**

- A financial statement that details income and expenses for the month.
- An intake report that describes the horses that have come into the organization. This information includes breed, age, abilities, and the reason for the animal's rescue.
- An adoption report that lists the number of horses available for adoption and adopted out. It also details the average length of time in rehabilitation, and how long it takes to find adoptive homes.

Bluebonnet also produces an annual report, which is published in a booklet format, and includes information on the rescue's activities for the previous year. It details the organization's financial information, including where monies came from and how they were used. It describes the various funds used to help the horses, such as our sponsorship fund, training fund, and the facility fund (which we hope will eventually purchase a permanent facility for the rescue). We use this report when we're trying to recruit corporate sponsorships, solicit large donations, or to request help from a law-enforcement group.

Event Planning

Another important task for your PR coordinator is to plan events, such as membership, adoption, or donation drives, in collaboration with the fundraising coordinator. Some events may last just one day, as in the case of an open house or transporting one of the horses to a pet store or horse show for public relations reasons; an adoption, membership, or donation drive can last anywhere from a week to a year.

When planning a drive, your PR person should plan for advertising as well as appearances on news shows. (Refer to "Press Kits" and "Advertising," on pages 75-76.) She should also encourage your membership to help recruit, and to ensure the event's success, should seek the assistance of several dedicated volunteers.

"Friend-raising" Booths

Putting up a booth at horse shows, pet fairs, equine expos, and other horse-related events is another way to raise awareness of your rescue's efforts. Bluebonnet uses booths to raise funds through the sale of various items and via donations. However, the main goal of these booths is to educate the public about horse rescue in hopes of attracting new volunteers and adopters.
Following is a list of what you'll need to set up a booth:

- One large table, two to three chairs, and a tablecloth (if not provided by the group hosting the event).
- Cardboard display boards. You can purchase these from craft stores. Look for the type that's divided into three sections and can stand on its own. Use the board to display your logo, some general information, and photos of some of the horses you've helped.
- Merchandise. Consider having T-shirts, polo shirts, and caps made with your organization's logo to sell at fund-raisers and booths.
- Brochures, information on membership, fostering, and adopting (including appropriate forms), and copies of your policies.
- Notebooks with photographs and information on the rescue's horses. Bluebonnet has a notebook of "success stories" along with photographs of horses that have been adopted. The rescue also has a notebook with information and photographs of horses that are available for adoption and those still in rehabilitation.
- A television and DVD or video player. At Bluebonnet's booth, we play DVDs and videos that include information about the organization, footage of our horses, and old news stories.

- And last, but not least, a donation jar. You may not get many donations, but sometimes Bluebonnet has been able to pay for the costs of the booth out of the money in the donation jar.

Finally, booths really aren't about fund-raising, they are about "friend raising." When you talk to visitors at your booth, you'll be recruiting supporters. They may not donate to your rescue or join the organization that day, but you'll hear from them anywhere from two weeks to two years later, when they want to adopt a horse or make a donation. You'll get your name out in front of horse people and horse-industry professionals, and they'll call your organization when they need a rescue, or know someone who does.

Outreach Programs

Community outreach programs are a terrific way to increase public awareness for your organization. They may target school groups, local horse clubs, 4-H and FFA clubs, and service-oriented organizations, such as women's groups, Girl and Boy Scouts, high-school honors groups, and sororities and fraternities. Your PR coordinator can contact these groups to introduce your organization and request to speak to their membership at a meeting. When speaking to horse clubs, 4-H and FFA groups, and college or high-school agriculture classes, your PR coordinator or another volunteer can discuss adoption and volunteering opportunities with attendees. When speaking to other groups, your PR coordinator may be able to recruit volunteers from the attendees to help your organization with fund-raising or other activities that don't require hands-on work with the horses.

As part of your outreach program, your organization can also participate in fund-raisers for other charities. Large organizations that do telethon fund-raisers on local PBS stations often need large groups of volunteers. This provides yet another way to get your name in front of the public and raise awareness of your organization. Bluebonnet sent volunteers to fill a phone bank at several PBS telethons. The host interviewed several of our members on television, mentioning our organization's name, and many others learned about the rescue.

Other organizations may need volunteers at walkathons, galas, or other events. In exchange for volunteering, your organization may be given a mention on TV or radio, or be allowed to set up a booth to distribute information.

Web sites

A Web site is another important tool to use for promotion. In fact, now that so many people have access to the World Wide Web, a Web site is a must. Many people turn to the Internet to research things they're interested in, find horses (to buy or adopt), and locate organizations they might wish to support. If you don't have a Web site, you're probably missing out.

When putting together a site, be sure to create one that's professional-looking, and that's easy to read and navigate. Start by securing a domain name—something like http://www.YourRescueName.org/. A domain name that's the same as your organization's name is easy for people to remember, and easy to place in ads, on business cards, and in your brochures or flyers. You can go to http://www.internic.com/whois.html to determine if the domain name you've selected is available. If it is, you'll need to purchase it through an Internet company that sells domains. (One that we use is www.godaddy.com.) They're usually cheap, only about $10 to $20 per year. After you've purchased your domain name, you'll need to select a company to host your Web site. This service runs about $10 to $20 per month, although you may be able to locate a company that'll donate the space. (*Tip*: The best and least expensive company I've found is one called Madbo. Go to http://www.madbo.com/.)

Once you've purchased your domain name and found a company to host your site, you'll need to decide what you want to put on it. Some organizations maintain a simple Web site that only provides basic information, such as the organization's mission statement and goals, pictures of rescued horses, and contact information. Other Web sites offer photographs and information about horses available for adoption, as well as information about adoption, donation, and volunteer opportunities. Some groups even allow you to apply online to adopt, foster, or volunteer; to file reports of abuse or neglect; or to make donations.

Bluebonnet offers a comprehensive Web page at http://www.bluebonnetequine.org/. It includes the following:

- General information about Bluebonnet Equine Humane Society
- Information about fund-raisers
- Contact information
- Biography of each director, officer, and staff member
- Financial information, including our IRS Determination Letter and 990s
- Answers to frequently asked questions (FAQs)
- List of volunteer opportunities
- List of policies
- List of forms
- Statistics on the horses taken in and adopted out
- Information and photos on each horse that's come into Bluebonnet
- Copies of each policy
- Forms to report abuse or neglect
- Applications for adopting and fostering
- General horse-related information
- Online "shop" where visitors can buy T-shirts, calendars, and ball caps.

In contrast, Creekside Farm Horse Rescue in Texas operates a simpler site at http://www.creeksidefarmhorserescue.org/. That site offers a list of horses and other animals available for adoption, a list of the rescue's needs,

> ## HOW TO MAKE THE INTERNET WORK FOR YOU
>
> In addition to having your own Web site, there are many other areas of the Internet you can use to promote your rescue. Here are a few suggestions:
>
> - Start an e-mail list to announce rescue events and to recruit local people who are interested in rescue.
> - Advertise the horses your group has available for adoption on one of the many equine Web sites that offer free advertising.
> - Add your Web-page address to the rescue lists online.
> - Look for Web sites that'll give you a free banner ad to help promote your rescue.
> - List information about your rescue and its available animals on PetFinder.org. This free site lists rescues across the country for dogs, cats, horses, and other species. PetFinder will give you a page to describe your rescue, and will also allow you to list horses available for adoption, along with a photograph, free of charge.

and membership and fostering information. The rescue operates a nice Web site that gives plenty of information about its horses and is easy to navigate.

With an idea in mind of what you want your site to say, your next task is to find someone to build and maintain your Web site. You may have someone in your volunteer ranks who has experience creating and maintaining Web sites. But if not, a willing volunteer can learn to create and edit Web pages. There are several online tutorials, and there are several Web-page editors that make the work much easier. There's also the option of hiring a Web-page programmer to create and maintain your site, but charges for these services vary greatly.

Regardless of who builds and maintains your site, be sure it's professional, easy to read, and loads quickly. Additionally, be sure to keep the information on your site up to date, and to include your address (including e-mail) and phone numbers on your Web page so that interested people can easily get in touch with you.

Newsletters

A monthly, bimonthly, or even quarterly newsletter is another great way to promote your organization, and to keep your members, volunteers, and sponsors up to date on what's going on. A newsletter can provide summaries of recent activities, such as adoptions and fund-raisers, and it can include a calendar of upcoming events, and a list of volunteer assistance you need. You can include photographs of horses you've recently taken in, as well as updates on those that have been adopted. Additionally, newsletters are a great way to generate outside interest in your group. Volunteers can leave copies of newsletters at feed/tack stores and veterinary offices, and you can hand them out whenever you have a booth at an event.

Expert's Tip

Jacalyn Ackerman, of the United States Equine Rescue League in North Carolina and Virginia, advises that you talk to your veterinarian, and any others in your area, about your rescue. He may be willing to give you discounted or even free services after being introduced to your group. But in addition to this, he'll also help spread the word about your group's efforts. He may tell people who are looking for a horse to contact you, and if he has a client who can no longer keep his horse, he'll send that client to you. Additionally, your vet can let you know about potential neglect situations.

PR – Your Biggest Task and Best Friend

As you can see, promoting your rescue is a very big job, and in addition to a good PR coordinator, you may want to recruit a committee of volunteers to assist him/her. But once you have a good public-relations program in place, your organization will benefit enormously as its name becomes more well-known, and volunteers, adopters, and donations begin to come your way.

Cloud

Cloud got her name because she was just about as easy to touch as a cloud when I got her. The local animal shelter had removed her from a negligent owner and then called us to see if we would take her. The catch? The mare was almost impossible to catch. She didn't lead, and she didn't load well. She also had cuts and scrapes on her legs, which she'd gotten from running through several barbed-wire fences while fleeing from the animal-control officers who'd come to save her. She was also emaciated.

I had no experience with wild horses, and wasn't really prepared to spend months taming one. But I couldn't turn my back on a horse in need, so I told them I would come get her. The shelter was able to get her into a corner and halter her for me, but she still wouldn't lead and we were only able to load her by parking the horse trailer at the end of an alleyway and running her into it.

Once we got her home, we ran her off the trailer and into a stall, and I began learning how to gentle a horse that had no interest in humans. Luckily, she wasn't terrified of humans (just uninterested), and within a few days she was eating out of a bucket that I held. Within a week, she was allowing me to rub her shoulder; and within a month, she'd gained weight and was looking better, and I started teaching her to lead.

Cloud was then moved into a foster home where she finished putting on weight and her caretakers taught her to trust humans. By the time she was adopted as an unridable pet, she led, allowed her feet to be handled, and stood to be groomed. Although she wasn't the type of horse I expected to foster, Cloud taught me a lot about the patience and persistence necessary to gentle horses that have never been handled.

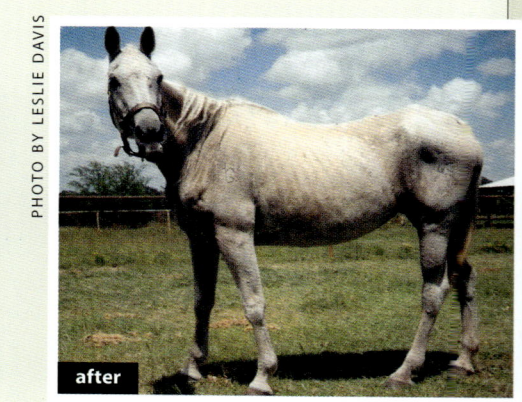

PHOTO BY JENNIFER WILLIAMS

before

PHOTO BY LESLIE DAVIS

after

seven

Get the Law on Your Side

It's absolutely crucial that you learn how to work effectively with law-enforcement officials.

A good working relationship with law-enforcement officials is essential if you plan to be involved in investigating reports of abuse or neglect and seizing horses. As a rescuer, you have no legal authority to remove horses from their owners, so you'll literally need the law on your side in order to see that neglected horses receive proper care. To begin, educate yourself—read the laws concerning abuse and neglect in your state (refer to "Know the Law," page 95). You need to understand exactly what constitutes abuse or neglect, and you need to know which city, county, or state authorities in your area are authorized to do something about it.

If you'll be operating within a city or town, you'll likely work with the police department, animal shelter, or humane society. If you'll be operating outside city limits, you'll probably be working with the sheriff's department. In some cases, animal shelters and humane societies also perform seizures throughout a county. Make a list of all the agencies you'll be working with so

DON'T MAKE PROMISES YOU CAN'T KEEP!

Before you attempt to align yourself with any law-enforcement agency, first make sure your rescue is fully prepared to assist in investigations and seizures. If you can't provide the requested assistance the first time the office calls for your help, you may not get a second chance. Here's what you'll need to have at the ready:

- Volunteers who are able to investigate neglect complaints and provide detailed reports
- Volunteers who can be ready to assist in a seizure, often on a weekday, with little notice
- A place to hold seized horses until a hearing or trial, when a judge (or justice of the peace) will determine what will happen to them. *Note:* In Texas, you may only need to hold horses for 10 days; in most other states, you may have to hold them for months.
- Room to accept horses into your rehabilitation program if a judge permanently removes them from their owner
- Funds to provide veterinary care for seized horses, and to rehabilitate them if they're released to your rescue. And be forewarned—you may spend thousands of dollars caring for horses only to have the courts return them to their owner.
- And last but not least, the appropriate knowledge to rehabilitate abused or starving horses (covered in Chapter 15, page 185).

you can contact them and get to know the people involved before you begin investigating complaints.

I've gotten the best response from the law-enforcement officers I've determined I want to work with by first contacting them and setting up a meeting. At these meetings, I introduce myself and the organization, and I may take the opportunity to introduce the officers to other rescue volunteers. I bring copies of the organization's IRS determination letter, brochures or fliers, our most recent newsletter, and any other information that I feel may be of interest to them. I then explain that my rescue is new to the area and that we plan to take reports of abuse or neglect, investigate those reports, and call the appropriate office when we discover horses in need. I describe how our group can assist them in the seizure of horses by providing trailers to transport them and a place to hold them until the court case, and by accepting them into our rehabilitation and adoption programs if a judge orders them to be removed from the owners.

Next, prepare for your meeting by making an outline that includes the benefits of cooperation between your rescue and their office. For example:

- You can save the officer's time by investigating reports of abuse and neglect to determine their legitimacy.
- You can provide volunteers with appropriate experience to assist the officer when he must seize a neglected horse.
- You can save the county money by transporting horses from the seizure location and impounding them.
- You can help prepare the case by documenting the condition of a neglected/abused horse, based on legally acceptable standards.
- You can collect statements from professionals regarding a horse's condition to help prove the case in court.
- The courts can award horses directly to your organization–saving the officer the additional time it would take to find homes or prepare the horses for auction.

7 | Get the Law on Your Side

If you or other members of your organization have any special training or experience that could assist law enforcement, be sure to emphasize that information. Volunteers with degrees in equine science, animal science, or veterinary science, especially those with advanced degrees, can serve as expert witnesses in court. If one of your members is a veterinarian, he may be able to provide veterinary care when a horse is seized, and then provide expert testimony as to the horse's condition. A member who's an attorney may be able to help the county attorney prepare the case. And volunteers who've been trained in the investigation and seizure of neglected/abused horses are an invaluable asset when working with law enforcement.

If all goes well with your initial meeting, the officer will be eager to learn more about your organization and may encourage others in his/her office to set up a formal working relationship. As a result, your rescue may become the official organization to seize neglected horses within that law-enforcement agency's jurisdiction. The agency may even offer your rescue a contract to perform specific duties, such as investigate local neglect reports, or accompany officers on neglect calls. Even if you don't receive a contract from the agency, the office may call you for assistance on a case-by-case basis. Keep in mind, the role your rescue will play in the cases in your area is up to the law-enforcement agencies involved. Therefore, it's important that you and your group make a good impression during your initial meeting.

Don't be discouraged, however, if the officer you meet with isn't willing to commit to working with your organization at that time. There may be several explanations for this: He may need to consult with his superior; his office may not have had any neglect cases, or he simply may not see the need to work with your group. In this case, thank him for meeting with you and let him know that you may contact him in the future if your organization receives a report of neglect within his jurisdiction. And if/when you do contact his office again, be sure to resubmit the information on your organization (the

IRS determination letter, flyer, or brochure, etc.) since they may not remember you from the first visit.

On the other hand, you may be surprised when that same officer contacts you a year or two later about a neglect case he needs help with, and you learn that he remembered you from that meeting.

Be Persistent and Patient

In some instances, law-enforcement officers have had to seize animals from rescuers who took in more animals than they could care for, or from animal collectors who called themselves rescuers. In other cases, officers may misunderstand the concept of rescue, believing that so-called rescue groups try to take horses away from good, caring owners whose horsekeeping practices simply aren't in line with their own (e.g., breeders, racehorse owners, or trainers whose methods they disapprove of). This can make many officers leery of working with rescues. Because of this, you may be asked for references from other law-enforcement agencies your organization has worked with in the past, or the agency may want to send someone to visit your facility to ensure that you can properly provide for the horses given into your care.

When I had been doing rescue for about a year, my group approached several sheriff departments and animal shelters in Texas to offer assistance in abuse and neglect cases. But the rescue's goal was to offer our services throughout the state of Texas, and we didn't yet have members in each county who could go meet, in person, with the various agencies and animal shelters. So, we mailed out packets of information to every sheriff's office, animal shelter, or humane society we could find. Our packets included information on the rescue, a copy of the Texas animal-neglect laws, and a letter explaining how we could assist their office.

After we'd sent out packets to the sheriff's offices, one of our members read that several horses had been recently seized in her county. We contacted animal control and learned that the horses had been awarded to the local animal shelter, which was seeking donations and adoptive homes for them. We called the animal shelter and set up a meeting to introduce ourselves and the rescue, and offer our assistance. At that time, the shelter authorities told us they had lined up adoptive homes for all the horses, but we might be able to work together in the future.

A few days later, the shelter called. It had just seized another horse who was several hundred pounds underweight, and who couldn't be caught or touched by animal-shelter volunteers. The shelter wanted to know if we could take the mare. While we didn't particularly want to rehabilitate a horse we couldn't even touch, we didn't feel we could say no since we had worked hard to set up a working relationship.

We took the mare, and in the process, developed a great relationship with that animal shelter, which enabled us to work together for the good of a lot of horses. The shelter called us whenever it seized horses, and we called to investigate reports of abuse or neglect in its county. The shelter remains a wonderful reference for us and has referred donors and adopters to us as well.

Generally, once you establish a working relationship with one law-enforcement agency or animal shelter, it becomes easier to establish relationships with others. It's important to build a reputation the right way—by being helpful and assisting officers when they need you. Your organization and volunteers will gain experience and knowledge from every officer with whom you collaborate, and those officers will often be happy to act as a reference for your group when you approach agencies in other cities or counties.

Additionally, the law-enforcement offices you work with may distribute information on your rescue to other offices that contact them asking for their assistance in investigating or seizing neglected horses. Remember, in most cases you can't seize horses on your own, so if you want to help them you need a healthy relationship with the law-enforcement officers who can.

What You Can Do for Law Enforcement

Once you establish a working relationship with a law-enforcement office in your area, there are many ways the two of you can work together, but the main way to assist the office you're working with is to take and investigate reports of neglect and abuse, assist with seizures, and help prepare cases for court. Let's take an in-depth look at each:

- *Take and investigate reports of neglect and abuse in your area.* The most likely ways in which you'll receive these reports are by telephone, e-mail, and at events you attend. However, be aware that these complaints aren't always legitimate. Sometimes people report their neighbors, or people they've done business with, after they've had a disagreement. I've investigated several such reports of neglect. In one such case, when I got to the location of the reported animals, I found healthy animals that appeared well cared for. Then, after talking to the complainant a second time, he told me about the problems he'd had with his neighbor, and it became quite clear that he'd made the report only to cause problems for him.

    In other instances, a person may report horses as neglected because he'd like to have the horses himself. This also has happened to me on several occasions. During the initial report of neglect, the complainants would tell me how much they loved the horses they're reporting, or how much they'd like to have them. They've even commented that attempts to buy those horses have been unsuccessful. Sometimes, they'll tell you if you'd just give them permission, they'd go pick up the horses and rehabilitate them for you, or they'll ask you to give them the horses after you've seized them. Then when a volunteer goes to check on the horses and their condition, she finds healthy horses.

    Because of these types of situations, it's our policy at Bluebonnet to tell complainants that to protect the safety of the horses we seize, we don't let neighbors adopt or foster them. If the complainant is reporting the horses because he or she wants them, the complaint is often dropped after hearing this. However, we still launch an investigation because we'd hate to mistakenly drop a report only to find out later that the horses were indeed suffering.

People also call in reports of abuse or neglect because someone isn't keeping horses the way they think they should be kept. The funniest neglect report I ever received was from a young girl. When I asked her what was wrong with the horse, she told me he was being kept in a "cage with bars," and was never allowed out. She was absolutely horrified, and I became concerned for his safety. (I envisioned a horse being kept in something that looked like a horse-sized wire dog crate.) As it turned out, the horse lived in a box stall in a barn, and he was taken out daily for exercise. But this young girl had never seen horses in stalls before, and she thought he was being cruelly confined in a cage.

Another person reported that her neighbors neglected their horses. When I asked why, she informed me that they didn't clean out their horses' hooves every day, and it was barbaric! I politely informed her that while we would prefer that horses had their feet cleaned out frequently, and even daily if possible, failure to do so did not constitute legal neglect.

When you begin taking neglect reports, you'll discover that probably 75 to 80 percent will fall into the above categories: disputes between neighbors, people who want someone else's horses, and people who disagree about acceptable horsekeeping practices.

Although only a few reports will probably turn out to be horses that really need intervention, you still must investigate them all. You don't want to jeopardize a horse's life because you didn't take a neglect report seriously. By conducting preliminary investigations to determine which reports are legitimate, you'll save the animal-control officers with whom you work a lot of time. These officers are often overworked and will appreciate anyone who can cut down the number of reports they have to investigate.

KNOW THE LAW

Before you investigate reports of abuse or neglect, you must know your state's animal-neglect laws, as well as what you can and can't do during an investigation. (*Note:* You can check with your state animal-control association to see if they offer classes on investigating neglect or abuse.) The Law Enforcement Training Institute at the University of Missouri-Columbia offers the National Cruelty Investigations School in conjunction with Code 3 Associates of Colorado. (Code 3 Associates is a group of attorneys, law professors, and former animal-control officers who train both animal-cruelty investigators and animal disaster relief.) The school consists of three levels, each involving a one-week workshop that's offered at various locations across the country. Topics include:

- **Understanding laws and the legal system**
- **Investigation procedures**
- **Documentation and collection of evidence**
- **Courtroom demeanor and testifying**
- **Veterinary reports**
- **Body-condition scoring of horses and other livestock**
- **Relationship of animal cruelty and humane violence**
- **Animal hoarders or collectors.**

While some parts of the classes are geared towards small animals, the courses teach volunteers the proper procedures for conducting investigations and seizures. Additionally, while attending these classes, your volunteers may make valuable contacts with city and county authorities who are willing to work with your rescue.

Code 3 Associates also offers an Equine Investigators Academy, which is conducted in both Virginia and Colorado, and involves an intensive week-long course. Half of this time is spent in classroom instruction, and the rest is hands-on with horses. The course includes information on the following topics:

- **Equine psychology and behavior**
- **Identification of horses**
- **Nutrition**
- **Body-condition scoring**
- **Veterinary care**
- **Disaster preparedness**
- **Loading and transporting horses**
- **Search and seizure**
- **Evidence collection.**

7 | *Get the Law on Your Side*

In many cases, neglect occurs due to ignorance–the owner may simply have jumped into horse ownership without knowing how to care for a horse or where to turn for help. In this type of situation, you may be able to work with the animal-control officer to educate the owner. A volunteer from your organization can accompany the officer to the property, meet with the owners, identify problems with the horses' care, and make recommendations for improvements (e.g., a new feeding regimen, regular farrier visits, or veterinary treatment). If the officer agrees, put the recommendations into an official format, including a statement that the owner agrees to make the proposed improvements, and have him sign it. Then, you and the animal-control officer will need to follow up with the owner in a few weeks, and if conditions haven't improved, the officer will need to obtain a warrant to seize the horses.

Note: I consider the greatest success in a neglect case to be when we can educate the owner, he improves the care of his horses, and he gets to keep them. I wish all cases were like this, and we never had to seize another horse.

- **Assist with seizures.** Often, the people in charge of animal control at police departments and sheriff's offices aren't trained to handle horses. Your volunteers can provide valuable assistance to these officers when there are neglected horses that must be seized. As I mentioned earlier, you should be able to provide a place to hold the horses from the day they're seized until a legal determination has been made as to their condition and what will happen to them. Also, you should have volunteers at the ready to transport horses because animal-control officers rarely have easy access to horse trailers. Additionally, volunteers with horse experience will be invaluable when it comes time to catch and load the horses during a seizure.

Note: Depending on your state, you may end up holding seized horses for months before the case goes to court. During that time, the horses do not belong to your rescue. Should it become necessary to euthanize a horse you're holding for a court case, you'll need to obtain a court order from a judge authorizing the euthanasia.

- *Help in the preparation of the case.* This is another way you can work with the officer in charge of animal-neglect cases. In addition to photographing the horses at the time of the seizure, you can assign body-condition scores, and go over them for signs of untreated injuries. You'll need to keep accurate records of any care given to the horses, and you'll need to document all veterinary and farrier care given to them. Your organization may also have access to a wider range of potential witnesses than would animal control, including veterinarians, farriers, trainers, and behaviorists, all of whom can provide statements describing the condition of the horses. These statements may be presented in court, or each professional may be called to testify to help prove a case of neglect.

At this point you may be wondering why you should work with law enforcement at all! In many cases, you and your volunteers will know more about horse care and handling than they do, and it might seem as though it would be easier to perform seizures on your own. However, remember that in most areas animal rescuers aren't allowed to seize horses without the assistance of law-enforcement officers. You'll need the law on your side to obtain a warrant, to serve it, and for legal access to private property to seize the horses. So don't ever forget that establishing a good, working relationship with the law-enforcement offices in your area is critical!

Crisco

We don't often see mules in the rescue—they are normally hardier than horses and can survive on much less food. So when we do get a neglect complaint involving mules, we worry since it normally means that there is absolutely nothing left for them to eat. Crisco's case was no exception: We found him and his eighteen pasturemates living in a wooded pasture with no grass.

Our volunteers arrived on the scene accompanied by several sheriff's deputies. Their goal was to round up the animals, get them loaded into trailers and take them to a safe place where they could receive food and veterinary care. However the animals were leery of the humans invading their home, and they slipped into the thick woods. The volunteers followed, shaking buckets of feed and trying to reassure the skittish creatures. After a while, one white mule emerged from the shadows. His backbone protruded and his ribs were easy to count. He was hungry, and he munched the grain a volunteer offered him.

Mules are slower to trust than horses, and they possess a strong memory for any wrong done to them. Crisco's previous owners had not been kind to him, so he did not trust his foster owner. Slowly she won him over and began working with him. Once he trusted his foster home, he learned quickly. Within months he was carrying a saddle and bridle and working in a round pen.

The shy little mule blossomed into a sleek, shiny character who loved attention and could be heard braying whenever anyone came by who might have a treat. He found an adoptive home quickly and is now a well-loved pet, spending his days hanging out with another mule and two ponies (all adopted from Bluebonnet), much loved by his adoptive "mom" and "dad."

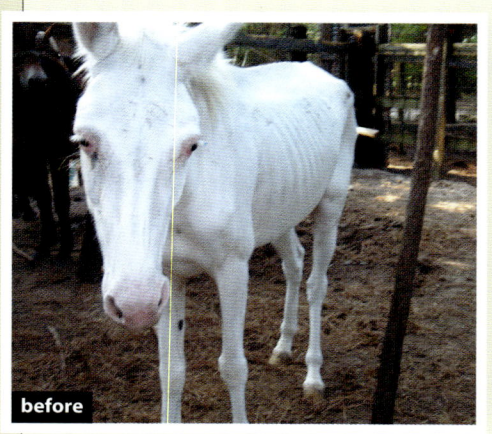

PHOTO BY JODI LUECKE

before

PHOTO BY BONNIE GULAS-WROBLEWSKI

after

eight

Fund-Raising

Your ability to do rescue work depends on your ability to raise funds. Here's how….

I n addition to veterinary, farrier, and feed bills, you'll need funds to pay for the rescue's business expenses, which include telephone, Web-site host, office supplies, and possibly employee salaries. Unless you're independently wealthy, or have a supporter who's willing to pay the rescue's bills, a fund-raising program is what will keep you afloat.

Unfortunately, fund-raising is not an easy task, and few people seem to enjoy it. The person you select as your fund-raising coordinator will play a vital role in your organization. Fund-raising takes time and dedication, and he or she needs to be committed to the job, detail-oriented, and able to recruit and manage volunteers to assist with events.

This person also needs to be thick-skinned. When I was in charge of fund-raising for a rescue, many of the members thought I put too great an emphasis on raising money. However, without a strong fund-raising program, we never would've been able to help the horses who needed us.

Any members, including officers and directors, who are willing to help with your fund-raising efforts can form a committee to develop and implement a fund-raising plan. Your coordinator should head up the committee, as she is the person who'll ultimately be responsible for its activities. As chairperson, she will lead committee meetings and discussions, and will assign fund-raising jobs to interested committee members. She should also obtain progress reports from the committee members, and she will need to fill in when someone is unable to perform her job.

When considering what individuals you want to serve on your fund-raising committee, willingness is the first criteria. Committee members must also be available to participate in various activities—they may need to take time off from work to help put on a fund-raiser, or spend their evenings and weekends planning and preparing events. Experience with fund-raising is definitely a plus, but people who are willing can always be trained.

The members of your fund-raising committee should understand and believe in your organization and its mission so they can intelligently discuss goals and answer questions when talking with potential sponsors. Also, enthusiastic, dedicated people will share their enthusiasm with potential contributors.

Additionally, members of the fund-raising committee can't be afraid to ask for money or other donations (a topic I'll cover in more detail later on). One of the best fund-raisers I've met asks everyone she meets to help the rescue—she asks for donations of feed, free advertising, even equipment. She often tells our members that the worst thing that can happen is they'll say no, and if they do, she knows there's always someone else she can ask.

Next, You Need a Plan

The first job for your fund-raising committee will be to develop a comprehensive plan. To begin, they'll need to determine how much money your organization is going to require. They can accomplish this by reviewing the rescue's annual budget or discussing needs with the board of directors. With this information in hand, the committee must consider the following as they work toward an overall plan:

The number of available volunteers. You don't want the committee to plan elaborate events only to discover they don't have the manpower necessary to make them successful.

Local laws. Before scheduling any events, the committee must research laws governing fund-raising in your state and city. Many states require you to register to solicit funds, and cities may require a permit before you hold an event. The secretary of state can tell you whether your rescue must be registered and can help you with the necessary paperwork. At the same time, ask the secretary of state's office for rules governing raffles. In Texas, only certain organizations are authorized to hold raffles, and in other states raffles are illegal. And during your research, don't forget to ask for guidelines on sales tax—some states require nonprofits to pay sales tax on all items they sell.

Promotional materials. Your fund-raising committee should work with your public relations coordinator to develop brochures and sponsorship packages designed to recruit donations. These promotional materials should include your mission statement and describe how your organization is unique from others. You might also include the costs of running the organization, as well as stories about individual animals. And, always include a plea for donations or sponsorships at the end.

Types of events. When you begin discussing the types of fund-raisers you'd like to put on, remember to diversify—set up some no-cost fund-raisers, but also invest in some of the bigger events. (For examples of all types of ways to raise money, see "Guide to Fund-Raising," on page 109.) Consider combining fund-raising ideas—hold a silent auction at your open house, or run a concession stand at a clinic you're hosting. Don't put all your hopes into one event or even one type of event. Try various types of functions and repeat those that bring in the most money.

If your organization is still small, consider contacting other nonprofit groups in your area to see about conducting a joint function. You can pool your resources and volunteers and split the proceeds. However, be sure to put in writing the expectations for each group, and the percentage of the proceeds they'll receive, before you begin organizing the event. While it may take careful coordination, working with another group to put on a fund-raiser is a great way to create strong ties to the community and bring in much-needed funds.

Once you've identified the types of fund-raising events your organization wants to hold, you'll need to lay out a schedule. I advise first setting up some ongoing fund-raisers, such as the affiliate programs or merchandise sales, and then proceed with the planning of events you can hold throughout the year. Space your functions carefully so you'll have sufficient time to prepare for each event, and don't forget to factor in the weather. Schedule your events at least three to five months ahead of time so your PR coordinator has enough time to plan an advertising campaign, and your fund-raising committee has time to recruit volunteers. Additionally, avoid scheduling so many events that you burn out your volunteers—give them plenty of time to rest and recuperate before it's time to begin working on the next one.

It's a Never-Ending Job

Fund-raising involves more than putting together and attending exciting events—soliciting donations is another aspect of fund-raising. As you may have noticed, I often suggest asking individuals or companies to donate items for events. If you're going to have a concession stand, ask a local grocer to donate hamburger patties, buns, and other supplies. If you need door prizes, approach local tack and/or feed stores to donate items. And if you're planning a horse show, ask the judge to donate his services. Every dollar you save is another dollar to care for the horses.

Many people new to rescue are intimidated (or even embarrassed) at the thought of asking for donations. Unfortunately, this is a part of fund-raising, and the worst thing that can happen is you'll be told "no." (*Tip*: Always remain cheerful and thank people for their time even when they turn you down. They may think about your request and change their mind, and your friendly attitude will make this an easy thing to do.)

On the other hand, if you develop a list of possible donors before you need to ask for their assistance, you'll receive less "nos" and more donations. Tell your friends, family, and people you do business with about the rescue. Share with them pictures and stories about the horses your group has helped. Let friends and family know about upcoming events, and invite them to meet the rescue horses and the volunteers. After you've spent time cultivating their interest in the rescue, let them know about a specific need–perhaps your group just seized some starving horses and you require funds for hay, or maybe one of the rescue's equine residents needs surgery. Explain what you need and why, then follow up with a request for donations, or challenge them to match your donation.

You can also generate interest and future donations from horse people you meet at your veterinarian's office or at horse shows. Be prepared to talk about the rescue and the horses' needs wherever you go–you may make new friends and donors for the rescue. I've handed out business cards to people I've met at the state fair, at horse shows, and even to someone I talked to while having my oil changed.

Once you've developed relationships with donors, remember to express your appreciation. Thank them whenever you receive a donation, and follow up with a handwritten thank-you note. If they donate towards a specific purpose, include a picture of what was accomplished; if their donation was for a specific horse, include a picture of the animal that will benefit from their act of kindness. You can also thank donors on your Web site and in your newsletter, and when holding events acknowledge those who made it possible in the event's program or over the public-announcement system.

You'll also need to send receipts for all donations, which you can include with thank-you notes. While the IRS only requires you to send out receipts for donations of $250 or more, it's a good policy to send a receipt for every donation. Your donors will appreciate being reminded of how much their assistance means to the rescue, and the receipts will help make recordkeeping easy. (Remember to keep a copy of each receipt for your organization's files, too.)

Now let's take a look at some of the different types of donations your organization may encounter, and how you should handle them.

In-kind donations. At some point, your organization will receive material donations, such as bags of grain, bales of hay, and possibly even a horse trailer or vehicle. Anyone who donates an item or items other than money needs to fill out two copies of an *in-kind donation* form. One copy goes to the donor and the other is kept by the rescue. This form should include:

- The organization's name and contact information
- The donor's name and contact information
- A description of each item that's being donated, and its value
- The donor's signature.

When a donor fills out an in-kind donation form, he's responsible for providing an accurate description of the donated item and its value. Your organization shouldn't assign values for donated items, and if the donor doesn't assign values you should leave them blank. The IRS does require that before a donor can claim a value of $5,000 or more for a donation he must have a qualified appraisal done prior to donation. The donor doesn't need to provide you with a copy of that appraisal, but he'll need it if he plans to claim the donation as a tax deduction. Make sure donors understand this restriction imposed by the IRS.

Quid pro quo donations. This type of donation consists of money that's given to the rescue partially as a donation and partially as payment for an item or services. The donor can only deduct the portion of the quid pro quo donation that's over and above the fair market value of the item or service received. For example, if a donor purchases a saddle from your organization that's valued at $200, but he writes his check for $500, he can claim $300 as a tax deduction (the amount on the check minus the value of the item purchased). You then need to issue a statement informing the donor of exactly how much he can claim as a tax deduction.

Grants. A grant is money awarded to special-interest groups by nonprofit organizations or foundations, or by some corporations. Generally, grants are awarded for a specific purpose, such as to develop a new program or expand an existing one, or to purchase new equipment. Some organizations, however, will provide grants for "general operating expenses," provided you're able to define exactly how you would use any grant monies you might receive (more on this in a minute).

Grants are often overlooked as a source of funds, because they require special effort. It takes time to research which foundations and corporations will award grants to groups like yours. Additionally, grant-writing requires good organizational and communication skills to clearly express the rescue's needs in grant applications, as well as an ability to precisely follow guidelines. But if you have the manpower available, grants can be an invaluable asset to your organization.

Before you start looking for a grant, you have to identify exactly what you want it to provide. It may be a stock trailer for transporting horses that have been seized, a round pen for training horses, or a set of portable panels so you can take a "spokeshorse" to events where he can meet the public. For these or similar needs, you'll look for a foundation that will award a grant for equipment purchases. Or maybe you need funds to purchase land where you can build your own rescue facility. In this case, look for a foundation that awards grants for land acquisition. If you need to make improvements to your facility, such as building a new barn or replacing the fencing, look for a grant for capital improvements.

There are also foundations that will award grants for "general operating expenses," which can include the specific costs of performing seizures, vaccinating the horses in your rescue, or paying for professional training for your horses in hopes of making it easier to find adoptive homes for them. A grant that provides funds to conduct an advertising campaign for a big event might also fall under "general operating expenses."

The Internet is a valuable tool for locating grants that may be suited for your rescue. Web sites like the Foundation Center at http://fdncenter.org/ provide databases of foundations and corporations that offer grants. Be sure to pay attention to the grant guidelines as they'll tell you what type of organizations the foundation will fund. For example, some foundations will only provide grants to nonprofit groups that promote the arts, while others only want to fund groups that promote animal welfare. There are also grants restricted to organizations located within a specific geographic region, and others only for specific needs, such as spay/neuter programs or general education. So, before you put the time and effort into writing a grant, make sure your organization and proposed program will qualify.

Once you've done your research and found a grant with guidelines your organization can satisfy, you'll need to determine what paperwork you must assemble. Some grants require you to complete an application, and others will provide you with a detailed list of paperwork you must submit along with a written proposal. Here are some tips to help you put together a grant package:

- *Follow the guidelines to the letter.* Make sure you include all required paperwork, answer any questions posed by the foundation, and write your grant proposal in the correct format.
- *Do your research.* Look at past grants made by the foundation—what types of organizations received them, and for what purposes? Also research the average amount of grants made in the past, and don't ask for more than that amount.
- *Demonstrate need.* You must convince the foundation that your organization has a strong need for the program, equipment, or funds your grant application describes. Explain how your rescue can function better once you receive the grant, and describe how your group's function is impaired without whatever it is you're seeking funds for.

For example, if you're requesting funds to purchase a stock trailer, explain that for your organization to effectively work with law enforcement you must be able to provide transportation for the horses their office seeks to remove from neglectful or abusive owners. You might also explain that neglected/abused horses often do not load well, and for this reason your current two-horse trailer isn't suitable for transporting such horses.

Explain the role of your organization. Tell the foundation why your rescue exists, and how it serves your community. If you work with law-enforcement officers to seize horses, describe your cooperative efforts and discuss how neglect cases were handled before your organization was formed.

If you plan to use grant-writing as a part of your overall fund-raising plan, you'll need to send out several grants each year. Not every grant you write will be funded, but the more proposals you send out the better your chances of receiving grant funds.

Fund-raising and the Bottom Line

The planning of a fund-raising schedule is a big and extremely important job. Your fund-raising committee is, in essence, directly responsible for bringing in the money that enables you to care for the horses, run the rescue, and hopefully expand the programs you offer so you can help even more animals. As you've learned in this chapter, there are many options for fund-raisers. To raise the most money possible, use as many different types of events as you can, and spread them throughout the year.

Guide to Fund Raising
Low- to no-cost events/programs

TYPE OF FUND-RAISER	Name-the-Horse Contest
HOW IT WORKS	For a nominal amount, say one dollar, you sell slips of paper upon which people can write their choice of a name for one of the rescue horses. (This contest can also be included in your newsletter.) At the deadline, you have a drawing to determine the horse's new name, and the winner is notified.
WHAT YOU'LL NEED	Volunteers to sell paper slips at tack shops, feed stores, etc.
UP-FRONT COSTS	Minimal (slips of paper)
INCOME POTENTIAL	Varies. The longer you let the contest run, the more slips of paper you can sell. Also the more volunteers you have selling paper slips, the more you can bring in. For a small organization, you may only make around $50—but that amount buys several bales of hay. Organizations with more volunteers can make several hundred dollars.
COMMENTS	This is a fun way to get people involved (especially kids) with almost no expense and little time. You can add to the fun by sending the winner a picture of the horse he named, along with updates on how the horse is doing in his foster home. A name-the-horse contest can also be used for foals that are born at the rescue.

TYPE OF FUND-RAISER	Horse-Sponsorship Program
HOW IT WORKS	Individuals can choose which horse they wish to sponsor (how—flyers, by visiting your organization's Web site or when visiting horses at your farm or at an event) with a one-time donation of $25, $50, or $100; or they can sign up for a monthly sponsorship of $25, $50, or $100, which is used to help pay for a horse's expenses on a continuing basis. Anyone who sponsors a horse is sent a receipt for their records, along with a photograph of the horse they've sponsored and a thank-you from him.
WHAT YOU'LL NEED	You'll need good pictures of any horses available for sponsoring. Putting moving stories about the horses and their needs on Web pages or flyers is a good way to get people interested.
UP-FRONT COSTS	Minimal. You'll need to cover the printing costs for the photos, but you can keep those costs down by printing the photos on your computer.
INCOME POTENTIAL	Varies depending on how strongly your rescue promotes its sponsorship program. We list our program on our Web site but do not heavily promote it. We bring in $100-$150 most months in sponsorships.
COMMENTS	This type of program allows individuals to take a personal interest in the rehabilitation of rescued horses, and can help pay for their care.

TYPE OF FUND-RAISER	**Affiliate Programs**
HOW IT WORKS	You sign up with the affiliate and list it on your organization's Web site. When items are purchased from your affiliates through a link on your Web site, you receive a predetermined percentage of the amount spent.
WHAT YOU'LL NEED	Someone to set up the program, which can take from 10 to 30 minutes, but then you're done—no maintenance is required.
UP-FRONT COSTS	None
INCOME POTENTIAL	Minimal, but can be steady
COMMENTS	Some affiliate programs require 501(c)(3) tax status, so be sure to read program requirements. Check out iGive, Amazon.com, and Jeffers Vet for affiliate programs.

TYPE OF FUND-RAISER	Corporate Sponsorship
HOW IT WORKS	Businesses help fund your activities in exchange for advertising on your Web site, a sponsorship banner displayed at fund-raising events, free admission to events, or complimentary T-shirts.
WHAT YOU'LL NEED	A comprehensive sponsorship package that includes: general information about your rescue and its need for funds, your organization's history, information about previous fund-raisers, information about any specific event for which you're soliciting funds (if applicable), and the benefits of purchasing a sponsorship (see "How it works").
UP-FRONT COSTS	Possibly gas and/or phone charges as you visit potential corporate sponsors. Printing costs for sponsorship package, unless copies can be made by one of your members.
INCOME POTENTIAL	Unlimited. While smaller companies such as a local business may give only $25-$100, large corporations may give $1,000-$5,000+. Getting the larger sponsorships takes time and research: You need to know who in the company to talk to and you'll likely need to meet with that person face to face.
COMMENTS	One benefit of a sponsorship program is that the monies can be spent wherever the rescue most needs it, unless you've received funds for a specific event. Plan on seeking corporate sponsorships six to 12 months before you'll need the money. At the very least, solicit sponsorships several months before an event because the amount of money you raise may determine the size of your event, as well as the amount of advertising and promotion you can afford. *Note: I've had the most success when I've solicited corporate sponsorships at the beginning of the year, as this is when many businesses are planning (and spending) their advertising and/or sponsorship budgets.*

TYPE OF FUND-RAISER	Direct-Mail Campaign
HOW IT WORKS	Most of us have received solicitation letters from such groups as the ASPCA and the Humane Society of the U.S. These letters often start with a touching story about animals the organization has saved, and may include a set of before-and-after photographs showing an animal that was saved. The letter usually describes the organization and why its work is important, and it concludes by asking the reader to donate funds to help the organization continue its work.
WHAT YOU'LL NEED	A mailing list. Collect the addresses of people interested in your rescue whenever you hold fund-raisers; your Web site can also invite visitors to e-mail their contact information to you so they can be added to your mailing list. *Tip: If you have the funds, you can purchase mailing lists from local horse magazines and tack/feed stores. Additionally, the ASPCA's Shelter Outreach program will provide a mailing list to local nonprofit rescue organizations.* http://www.aspca.org/site/PageServer?pagename=pro_shelter-outreach
UP-FRONT COSTS	Printing letters (unless a members can make copies); postage; possible purchase of a mailing list; envelopes. *Note:* You can pay companies to send out bulk mailing like this, but make sure to research the costs. They can vary greatly.
INCOME POTENTIAL	Solicitation letters offer a low return rate—between one and five percent of people who receive such letters actually make a donation. *Tip: If you use solicitation letters to raise funds, be sure to send out enough to make the effort pay off.*
COMMENTS	Be sure to personalize these letters by including some of your rescue stories and/or photos. The letter should be from your president or vice president, and should explain why you're asking for money, and why your need is urgent. Include a return mailer and a form for donors to fill out that includes how much they're donating, and how they'd like their money spent (e.g., veterinary bills, seizure expenses, or training volunteers to be better prepared during seizures).

8 | Fund-Raising

TYPE OF FUND-RAISER	Grant-Writing
HOW IT WORKS	Nonprofit organizations, foundations, and some corporations award funds to special-interest groups for a variety of purposes.
WHAT YOU'LL NEED	A person with good organizational and communication skills, who has the time required to research and write grants.
UP-FRONT COSTS	Minimal. Unless you decide to hire a professional grant writer.
INCOME POTENTIAL	Depends on the grant. Some foundations only award $500-$1,000. Others award millions of dollars. **Note:** The smaller grants are much more common and not generally as competitive as the big grants. Inexperienced nonprofits ought to get some experience writing smaller grants before hitting up those foundations who do the large ones.
COMMENTS	Grant-writing is time-intensive, but can be an invaluable asset to your organization. Refer to the section on "Grants," page 101, for in-depth information. Also once you get one grant, future grants are often easier to get. Foundations like to know they're funding an organization that other foundations have trusted in the past. Many grant applications ask for you to provide a list of all grants awarded to the organization in the past.

TYPE OF FUND-RAISER	eBay, for online auctions
HOW IT WORKS	eBay (www.ebay.com) works with MissionFish (www.missionfish.org) to allow nonprofit organizations to set up accounts to list items in online eBay auctions. Proceeds from the sale of these items will go to your organization. Additionally, your members and supporters can sign up to sell items through MissionFish. When they do, they can designate that a portion of the sales price goes to your rescue.
WHAT YOU'LL NEED	Someone to manage the listings, collect payment, and handle shipping of items you list for sale
UP-FRONT COSTS	eBay listing fees, which depend on a lot of factors: starting bid for the auction, reserve bid for the auction, and final selling price. These fees are usually between 3 and 7 percent of the final selling price when you sell your own items.
INCOME POTENTIAL	Can be significant, depending on how aggressively you solicit donated items to sell online.
COMMENTS	Because this online site reaches all kinds of people, with varied interests, you're not limited to horsey items—you can sell anything.

TYPE OF FUND-RAISER	Paypal (www.paypal.com), for online credit-card processing
HOW IT WORKS	You set up an account, which enables you to receive credit-card payments for items purchased online from your Web site.
WHAT YOU'LL NEED	Someone to set up your account
UP-FRONT COSTS	None, but you will be charged a percentage of your sales
INCOME POTENTIAL	N/A; depends on sales/purchases
COMMENTS	Paypal buttons on your Web site enable visitors to "impulse shop" or "impulse donate" using their credit card. Bluebonnet also uses Paypal for membership payments. We feel the percentage that Paypal charges is a small price to pay to bring in these funds. You'll also have the convenience of using your Paypal account for online purchases for the rescue.

One-person events

TYPE OF FUND-RAISER	Dinner or Barbecue
HOW IT WORKS	You tell your friends you're hosting a dinner to raise funds for your rescue and invite them to attend. Hand out membership information on your rescue and ask for donations.
WHAT YOU'LL NEED	Members willing to host such events
UP-FRONT COSTS	None
INCOME POTENTIAL	In our experience, the most we've received is $400, but it could be more if you have a member with a lot of friends to invite to the dinner.
COMMENTS	The hostess can also offer homemade baked goods for sale, in addition to asking for donations.

TYPE OF FUND-RAISER	Challenge Campaign
HOW IT WORKS	Donate $50 to your rescue and challenge all your friends and relatives to do the same. You can also send out pictures of a specific horse and ask those on your list to match your donation to help pay for special medical treatment.
WHAT YOU'LL NEED	Willing members and supporters
UP-FRONT COSTS	None
INCOME POTENTIAL	Varies
COMMENTS	Several Bluebonnet members have done this and raised several hundred dollars each.

8 | Fund-Raising

TYPE OF FUND-RAISER	**Christmas or Birthday Donations**
HOW IT WORKS	Instead of buying your friends and family gifts, make a donation to the rescue in their name and ask them to do the same for you. For older kids (who can benefit from a lesson about giving), consider setting up a birthday party with a request that donations be made to the rescue in lieu of presents.
WHAT YOU'LL NEED	Willing members
UP-FRONT COSTS	None
INCOME POTENTIAL	In our experience, the most we've received has been $500—but other rescues may get more depending on how many people participate.
COMMENTS	Don't forget to have someone in your organization send out notification cards to those who've had donations made in their name.

Large events

TYPE OF FUND-RAISER	Walk-a-thon, Pet Walk, or Marathon
HOW IT WORKS	Participants may either pay an entry fee or get sponsors who agree to donate a certain amount (example: $1) for each mile walked or run.
WHAT YOU'LL NEED	A place where you can hold the event; authorization from city officials if you plan on using city streets; volunteers to mark out the route, distribute maps/courses, register participants, hand out prizes, and answer questions; an EMT on site; an on-call veterinarian if animals are involved.
UP-FRONT COSTS	Advertising and prizes for participants. *Tip: You may be able to find local businesses that are willing to donate prizes.*
INCOME POTENTIAL	Varies depending on the size of the event—with enough participants, your organization may raise several thousand dollars.
COMMENTS	The advantage of these types of events is their wide appeal—both horse people and nonhorse people can participate and have fun.

TYPE OF FUND-RAISER	Trail Ride
HOW IT WORKS	Participants pay a fee to ride in the trail ride.
WHAT YOU'LL NEED	An appropriate area, such as a state park with good trails, or you might be able to access ranch land through a member or contacts you've made; an EMT on site during the ride, and a veterinarian who's willing to be on call; volunteers to lead the ride, register riders, and serve lunch.
UP-FRONT COSTS	Advertising—to reach as many riders as possible, you'll need to run ads in horse magazines, newspapers, and the newsletters for any local trail-riding groups; lunch for hungry riders. *Tip: You may be able to get local restaurants or grocery stores to donate lunch items.*
INCOME POTENTIAL	Several hundred to several thousand dollars
COMMENTS	This type of event obviously has a narrower appeal than other events because it's only open to horse owners.

TYPE OF FUND-RAISER	Merchandise Sales
HOW IT WORKS	You have T-shirts, sweatshirts, baseball caps, and other items printed with your logo, then sell them on your Web site and at local events.
WHAT YOU'LL NEED	A logo that reprints well and someone who can make items for you—check with local printing companies, silk-screening companies, etc.
UP-FRONT COSTS	The cost of your first order, but after that you can reinvest your proceeds in additional merchandise
INCOME POTENTIAL	Slow, but fairly steady
COMMENTS	Consider asking an artist to donate a painting or drawing of rescue horses to put onto T-shirts. These shirts can be gorgeous, and give your supporters more options to choose from when they're looking for something to purchase.

TYPE OF FUND-RAISER	Garage Sale
HOW IT WORKS	Members and volunteers donate and collect items for a one-day sale.
WHAT YOU'LL NEED	A location, such as the front yard of someone's house or your rescue facility; items donated by members; volunteers to collect and price items, as well as work the sale.
UP-FRONT COSTS	Advertising to bring in buyers.
INCOME POTENTIAL	Depends on the energy of those involved. There is potential for $1,000+ depending on how many donated items you get and the quality of the items.
COMMENTS	Bluebonnet held a garage sale on a Saturday in the parking lot of a local feed store that also contributed to the cost of advertising. Members collected horse and farm items, tools, furniture, and other household items. They raised around $1,500 for the rescue.

8 | Fund-Raising

TYPE OF FUND-RAISER	Bake Sale or Concession Stand
HOW IT WORKS	Ask a local horse club to allow you to have a concession stand at one of its shows.
WHAT YOU'LL NEED	Baked goods; sandwich items and drinks; a table and tablecloth; a banner; one or two volunteers to run the stand, depending on the size of the show.
UP-FRONT COSTS	Minimal (see comments)
INCOME POTENTIAL	Up to $1,000
COMMENTS	Members can make or donate most items (the show facility may have a table). Be sure to check with the local Department of Health to make sure you don't need a health permit or other paperwork.

TYPE OF FUND-RAISER	Open House
HOW IT WORKS	If your rescue has its own facility, you open it to the public for a specified period of time.
WHAT YOU'LL NEED	Plenty of volunteers to host and manage the event. Consider recruiting educational speakers, such as a veterinarian or farrier, to address health issues and proper horse care.
UP-FRONT COSTS	Advertising in horse magazines and local newspapers
INCOME POTENTIAL	Minimal (donations from attendees)
COMMENTS	This type of event requires a lot of work and isn't inexpensive to put on. The main benefit is increased awareness of your group's efforts and needs. Send out press releases to all local media, including radio and television. You can also ask local businesses to donate door prizes.

TYPE OF FUND-RAISER	Phantom Event
HOW IT WORKS	An example of a phantom event is a "Tea Party in an Envelope." You send supporters and friends an invitation (complete with tea bag) that says: "This is an invitation to a tea party—one you can have anywhere you like. Just remember to send us a donation when you have your party!"
WHAT YOU'LL NEED	Volunteers to put together the mailing
UP-FRONT COSTS	Printing/postage for invitations
INCOME POTENTIAL	Can bring in thousands of dollars throughout the year
COMMENTS	Be creative with your phantom event—the more fun and clever you make it, the more people will participate. Great return on a minimal investment.

TYPE OF FUND-RAISER	Riding, Training, or Health-Care Clinic
HOW IT WORKS	Find a local trainer/clinician, veterinarian, or farrier who's willing to donate his/her time, or bring in a nationally known clinician, and charge for participation (higher rates are charged for those participating with their own horse) as well as auditing.
WHAT YOU'LL NEED	A facility to hold the clinic; volunteers to help register attendees, assist the speaker, and answer questions
UP-FRONT COSTS	Advertising in local horse magazines and newspapers.
INCOME POTENTIAL	$300 to $500. When you bring in a regionally or nationally known clinician, you make a lot more—there is the potential for several thousand dollars.
COMMENTS	If you have enough volunteers, consider having a concession stand to raise additional funds.

TYPE OF FUND-RAISER	Horse Shows or Play Days
HOW IT WORKS	Your rescue hosts and organizes either a one-day open horse show or a one-day play day. Another option is to partner with an established show or play-day association to put on an event to benefit both organizations.
WHAT YOU'LL NEED	Several volunteers to manage the show/play day. You may also want to offer a concession stand as another way to make money.
UP-FRONT COSTS	Fees for an arena, judge's compensation, ribbons or other awards, printing a schedule of events, and advertising.
INCOME POTENTIAL	Up to $2,500 per show
COMMENTS	You may be able to get arena fees waived, and you may be able to find a judge willing to donate his services. Also, ask local businesses to donate items for prizes, or use their donations for a silent auction or as door prizes. If you have enough volunteers, consider having a concession stand to raise additional funds. *Note:* Bluebonnet is putting together a series of open horse shows that will include classes specifically for rescue horses, and will offer high-point awards for each show, as well as high-point for the series.

TYPE OF FUND-RAISER	Auction
HOW IT WORKS	You can hold either a live or silent auction, and it's not too hard to get local businesses, supporters, and members to donate items. You can limit the auction to only horse-related items, or you can include jewelry, ranch/farm equipment, and household items. For a silent auction, people write their bids on paper during a set amount of time (often somewhere between one and four hours).
WHAT YOU'LL NEED	A place to hold it (unless it's online); and for a live auction, a good auctioneer to excite participants and encourage them to keep bidding.
UP-FRONT COSTS	Advertising; and it's worth a little added expense, if necessary, for a professional auctioneer.
INCOME POTENTIAL	Varies depending on the number and quality of items donated.
COMMENTS	A good auctioneer will take advantage of breaks in the action to remind the audience about your organization's mission, and can invite you to bring some horses on stage so the crowd can see firsthand the animals they're helping.

Madison

Madison was removed from her negligent home in a cooperative effort between the local sheriff's department and our rescue. When we first met her, she was so thin and weak that we weren't sure she could recover. The first night Madison was safe she laid down to rest, but was too weak to get back up. Luckily several strong volunteers helped Madison rise, but for the next week they had to repeat the same routine: Madison would be down in the morning, unable to stand on her own, and they would help her back to her feet.

As Madison gained weight, she also regained her strength. After a week of plentiful, healthy food, Madison was able to get up on her own after lying down.

Madison's health improved and her beautiful brown and white coat began to shine, but she remained aloof and distant from her caretakers. She was hard to catch, and she refused to look at her handlers. However, if Madison's handler ignored her, she'd watch her handler—seeming to long for attention. We wondered what had happened to her, and we wondered if she'd ever learn to trust humans again.

When Madison was healthy enough to ride, she moved to a new foster home. Her caretaker loved Madison's spirit and didn't mind that she loved to go fast, and sometimes crow-hopped or even bucked when she was held back. She loved Madison and decided to adopt her.

What's even more exciting is that Madison seems to love her new person, too. She'll let her adopter catch her and pet her, and she seems to love the attention. Madison has finally found a human she can love and trust.

PHOTO BY SPENCER WILLIAMS

before

PHOTO BY REGINA ANDERSON

after

nine

The Value of Networking

Increase the number of horses you can help by joining forces with other caring groups.

Every month, there are thousands of horses throughout the United States that need help and no one organization can rescue them all. However, when rescue groups join forces they can increase the number of horses each group can help by sharing resources, collaborating during large seizures, and providing support for each other. For example, if you don't have room for an owner-released horse, you can refer the owner to another organization. Similarly, if you don't have a horse that would meet a specific adopter's needs, you can still help a rescue horse find a home by referring that person to another group. Everybody wins.

With the obvious advantages of networking, you might think that all rescues work with other groups. However, networking among rescues seems surprisingly rare. Too often, those who run rescues have the attitude that they're in competition with other groups for funds and other resources, and they fear that working together will result in a loss of members, donors, and adopters. But this kind of thinking benefits no one—least of all the horses in need. Instead, both rescues need to remember that the horses come first–protecting all equines from danger, removing them from neglectful owners, rehabilitating them, and placing them in good adoptive homes is more important than the benefits to any one organization.

Keep an Open Mind and Heart

Sometimes rescues don't work together because they have different philosophies. A rescue that doesn't allow its adopted horses to be resold may refuse to work with a rescue that turns over full ownership of its horses to adopters. Or a rescue that specializes in purchasing needy horses from auctions may not see any reason to network with a group that focuses on seizing equines from neglectful homes.

As you learned in the first chapter of this book, there are many different ways to set up a rescue. I believe that as long as the rescue is honest about how it operates, honest with the groups it works with, and cares for its horses, it is doing a good job helping horses. So when it comes to considering whether or not you're going to network, don't refuse to work with an organization just because its policies aren't exactly the same as yours.

Bluebonnet cooperates with Creekside Farm Horse Rescue and Hopeful Haven Equine Rescue Organization, and is working to establish relationships with other rescues as well. These groups are very different. Creekside existed for about three years before Bluebonnet was founded, and I worked with Creekside's president, Judith, before setting up Bluebonnet. Creekside operates as a private rescue, with Judith and her husband providing funds out of their own pocket, whereas Bluebonnet was founded as a nonprofit group. While Creekside is regional, operating only in northern and eastern Texas, Bluebonnet strives to cover the entire states of Texas and Arkansas.

Although these rescue programs are different, we work well together.

Judith and I offer each other emotional support, often calling each other when the going gets tough. It's hard to completely understand the rigors of rescue unless you're in the trenches, and we can sympathize with each other. Sometimes we offer suggestions, and other times we simply listen, allowing the other to vent. This mutual support gives each of us someone to turn to, and provides the encouragement we need to keep going.

Networking with other rescues can provide you with moral support and camaraderie, too. Rescue work can be very demanding physically and emotionally. It can take up all your free time, making burnout common among rescue workers. Having someone to talk to who understands what you're going through can be a tremendous help. When you work closely with another organization, you have access to more people who realize how difficult rescue can be. They can offer not only emotional support, but also physical help with the rescue if you become injured or simply need a brief break.

In addition to this, both our rescues take reports of neglected and abused horses, and we each work with law-enforcement agencies to get help for needy horses. If we receive a report of neglect in Creekside's area, we ask them to investigate. When they have a neglect case that's too big for them to handle alone, we send volunteers and assistance their way. Working together, we can help more horses than either one of us could by working alone.

Bluebonnet also works with other rescues. We offer advice to help new rescues get started. In fact, I decided to write this book after receiving multiple e-mails from people looking for help with starting a rescue. We also advise new rescues on how to investigate reports of neglect, and have offered to assist them with seizures and court preparations. When people who live out of our area contact us to donate a horse, adopt a horse, or volunteer, we often refer them to rescues in their area. We help other groups inspect potential adoptive homes that are located within our area, and we've worked with other rescues to check up on some of our adoptive homes. Occasionally we have horses that

9 | The Value of Networking

need to be relocated due to health problems, such as heaves (a respiratory problem) or anhidrosis (the inability to sweat). These horses need a cooler, dryer climate than Texas, and through networking with other rescues, we can find suitable homes for them in other areas.

A group of horse rescues in Virginia has formed a loose network. They work together to investigate reports of neglect, and when multiple horses are seized, several rescues in the network cooperate to execute the seizure and house the horses. They help each other transport horses, and when one rescue is too full to take in a donated horse, they refer the owner to one of the other rescues. Chris Smith, of Travelers Rest Equine Elders Sanctuary, says that because the rescues pull together they're able to help more horses than they could on their own.

Double Your Funds

As you can see, by working together your rescue and other groups can help a greater number of horses get into good homes than you could accomplish working solo. But there are other benefits of networking, too. Many foundations like to award money to organizations that collaborate on projects. If you work with other rescues you can combine efforts and write a large grant to go after some of these funds.

Networking with other organizations can also enable you to collaborate on a bigger fund-raiser than your group could handle alone. Together, you can pool resources, such as contact lists, volunteer manpower, and finances. Your organization may have an experienced fund-raiser with the skills to put an event together efficiently, while another organization may have an experienced public-relations person who's a whiz with advertising. A large fund-raiser can bring in more funds than the small, simple fund-raisers that each group would put together on its own.

Caveat: If you decide to work with another organization to conduct a joint fund-raiser, put all your plans in writing. Include how much volunteer manpower and money each group will contribute, and define what percentage of the proceeds will go to each one. If you do this in advance, you'll avoid the possibility of miscommunication.

Look Before You Leap

Before you discuss networking with other rescues, there are a few cautions. Not all rescues are well-run. If your group is linked with a rescue that has a bad reputation in the community, your organization's reputation may be damaged, too. People may confuse your groups, or they may believe that because you work together your group endorses or employs the same practices that earned the other organization its bad reputation. So do your homework before collaborating on projects or assisting another rescue.

Start by talking to the head of the rescue several times, and then meet in person, if possible. If the organization has a facility, visit it. Is it clean and well-run? Is it suitable for the number of horses housed there? Do the horses look healthy and happy? Are there any that are injured, ill, or underweight, and if so, are they receiving the attention they need to recover? If the organization uses

Expert's Tip

Jan Carter, of S.C.A.R.E. (South Carolina Awareness and Rescue for Equines) in South Carolina, hasn't yet had the chance to network with other rescues because there are so few in her area, but she believes networking is important. According to Jan, "If two rescues have equally good reputations there should be no barriers to them coming together to provide better services to their area. I look forward to the chance to work with other groups in the future."

9 | The Value of Networking

foster homes, ask what qualifications they require. Also ask how they check up on their foster homes to make sure they're providing good care for the horses. And what do they do if it's determined that a horse isn't working out in a particular home? Finally, expect the other rescue to check you out as well.

Ask the rescue about other organizations or agencies they've worked with in the past. Call those groups and inquire about their experiences with the rescue in question. Ask for details on how the two groups have collaborated, and their overall impression of the group. Ask if they would work with the rescue in the future—and if not, why?

While you may be excited about networking now, don't forget the caveats mentioned above. After careful consideration, I hope you do decide to network with other organizations. Compile a list of equine rescues and sanctuaries in your area. Include other organizations that take in horses, such as farm-animal sanctuaries or animal shelters. If you don't have any rescues in your area, look for organizations throughout your state, or even in surrounding states. You can also find rescues by searching the Internet, looking in the phone book, or talking to your local animal shelter or animal-control officer. You may even hear about organizations on the news or see them in the newspaper.

Expert's Tip

Jorg Huckabee-Mayfield, of White Bird Appaloosa Horse Rescue in Virginia, says, "Our rescue works with others that have a good record of properly caring for their horses and tracking where they end up. We don't want to be associated with a rescue that appears to be brokering or breeding their horses." He goes on to add, "We also don't want to get involved in infighting between rescue groups, so we tend to avoid those with a history of fighting with others."

Next, do your homework before contacting the groups you find. Talk to people in your community to see if they've heard anything about the rescue or worked with it. Look over the organization's Web site and request information from it. Check with local newspapers to see if the rescue has been featured in any articles.

After you've done some research, e-mail or call the organizations on your list. Introduce yourself and your rescue, and explain that you're contacting other groups that work with horses in hopes of developing a network. Explain that you believe you can help more horses by working together. Set up a time to meet with rescue representatives, see their facility, talk about their rescue operations, and discuss how both groups, and the animals they help, can benefit by networking. *Note:* If there are several rescues in your area, try to set up a meeting with all of them. You may be able to form a coalition where all the groups work together.

When you've met with the directors and presidents of the other rescues in your area, you'll need to decide which group(s) you think you can work with. Consider how each organization's facility looked and how they ensure that their foster horses get proper care. Consider each organization's reputation in the community and how other agencies feel about them. Examine each group's policies, but don't allow a difference in opinion to completely turn you away from networking with a particular organization.

Here's a good example: Bluebonnet doesn't believe in adopting out rescue horses to be used as breeding animals, and we don't let our adopters sell horses they adopt from us (they must be returned to us). However, we'll still work with rescues whose policies differ from ours. We can collaborate on abuse and neglect investigations, put on joint fund-raisers, and perform seizures together. Bluebonnet sometimes seizes more horses than we can easily accommodate. When that happens, we'll transfer some of them to other rescues–but only those with acceptable adoption policies. While we won't transfer horses to a rescue that allows breeding or resale of its animals, we can still work with those rescues on other projects.

Another decision you'll need to make is whether or not to work with private rescues. White Bird Appaloosa Horse Rescue doesn't believe 501(c)(3) status is necessarily indicative of a good rescue, so that group is willing to work with private rescues and individuals. Bluebonnet will work with private rescues to investigate reports of neglect and perform seizures, but we generally choose not to transfer horses to private rescues because they have less public accountability.

Networking Can Benefit Everybody

When used carefully, networking allows several organizations to help more horses than they could alone. Working together will also enable you to hold larger fund-raisers and handle larger seizures than you could by yourself, and it may help get more horses placed into great homes. Another plus is that many foundations award grants specifically to organizations that collaborate with others. If your organization can work with another to write a joint grant, you'll increase your chances of getting the grant. Just remember: Thoroughly check out any organizations you're thinking about working with. A good reputation is hard enough to earn, but a bad one is almost impossible to repair.

Logan

Logan was part of one of the worst neglect cases our rescue has ever been involved in. The sheriff's department received a complaint of neglect and called us to help them remove the horses. When our volunteers arrived, they discovered five donkeys, seven mules, and seven horses. Even worse, they discovered four dead equines—one of which had its back legs tied together. Although the volunteers were disgusted and horrified by what they saw, and many wanted to sit down and cry, they realized there were living horses that still needed their help.

The horses hadn't known kind treatment in the past, so they weren't easy to catch, halter, or load. But they were hungry, so they followed food into the trailer. The next day they were put into a chute so our veterinarian could draw blood for a Coggins test, and that's when a volunteer discovered that Logan was a BLM mustang. With help from the BLM, we discovered that Logan had been captured in Nevada and adopted over a year ago. The BLM

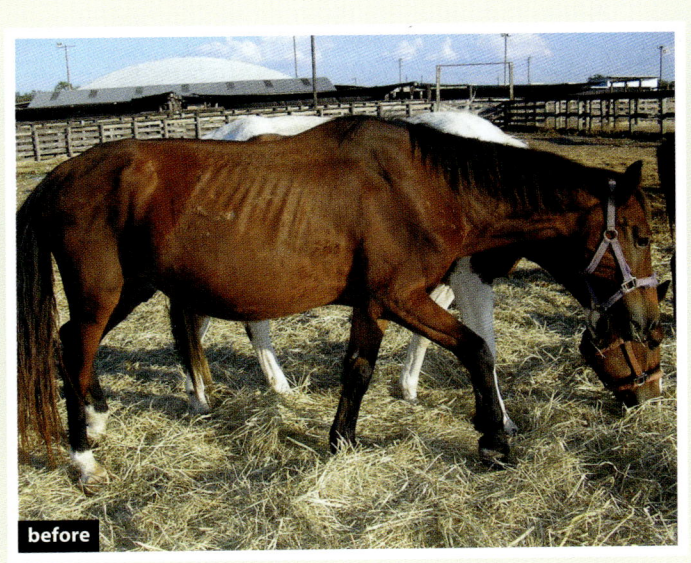

before

PHOTO BY SPENCER WILLIAMS

only tracks mustangs for one year after their adoption, when the owners are given titles. So no one knew how Logan ended up where he was until his negligent owner stated that he'd bought Logan and the other animals at local auctions.

When Logan moved into his foster home, no one could touch him. His foster "mom" quietly and slowly worked with him until she could halter him in his stall, and he'd let strangers pet him. She began grooming him and taught him to pick up his feet, and then one day she saddled him. Since he seemed to accept the saddling process and willingly walked, trotted, and cantered around the round pen, she climbed up on his back. She found that Logan was broke to ride and she began riding him daily.

Logan is still wary of new people, and he may never completely lose that mustang trait. But he's now safe, healthy and happy—and he's even learned to enjoy hugging and grooming from his foster mom.

PHOTO BY JENNIFER WILLIAMS

after

ten

Create Community Support

"Charity begins at home" is especially true when it comes to rescue work.

Community support is critical to the success of nonprofit organizations. Where that support comes from will be determined by the scope of your organization. For example, if your organization will provide services to an entire state, you'll be able to seek support from a much larger area than if you only provide services to a city or county. While those rescues serving a limited region have a restricted area from which to draw support, they also have the chance to get to know people in their community much better than rescues that are more spread out.

There are many good reasons to network within your community, not the least of which is support when you have an emergency. In these instances, I've seen communities pull together to help rescue groups feed, house, and care for starving horses. People have donated thousands of dollars to ensure that horses and other animals got necessary surgeries and medical care—all because the rescues that cared for the animals had worked to develop a solid base of community support before there was a dire need.

Through networking and fund-raisers, you can find donors, volunteers, and potential adopters in the area you serve. Members of the community may offer invaluable services to your rescue—you could meet an accountant, public-relations expert, or an attorney who's willing to work with your rescue for a reduced rate.

This is where your public-relations coordinator comes in (see Chapter 6, "Public Relations," page 69)—in order for you to network within your community, its members must know about your organization. You can get your name out there by setting up information booths at local events, advertising in local newspapers, and by distributing flyers and brochures. You can also send press releases to all local media, and request that local radio and television stations run public-service announcements about your group.

When you consider working within the community, keep in mind that this is a give-and-take relationship. Your rescue is providing a community service by helping neglected horses, as well as taking in horses whose owners can no longer provide for them. However, your commitment to the community should extend beyond the services your rescue offers. Following are some of the many other ways in which you can become involved in your community.

Service-learning programs. In these programs, high-school or college students learn how to apply skills they've learned in school to real-world situations. For your rescue, agricultural students could put together a better design for your rescue facility, or formulate balanced grain rations for your horses; business students could develop a long-range business plan or organize a fund-raiser; and education students could develop a program to teach younger children about horses or animal welfare. At the same time students are getting valuable hands-on experience, your organization benefits with new programs and/or improved care for your horses.

Community-service programs. Many communities need organizations that offer community-service programs. Some high schools and colleges require their students to complete a set number of community-service hours before graduation, and the courts sometimes sentence offenders to mandatory community service. Your organization can provide an opportunity for these people to fulfill their obligations.

While those seeking community-service hours may not know anything about horses, you can put them to work cleaning pens, building or repairing fences, or repairing buildings. They can help out at fund-raisers, maintain your Web site, or work to promote the rescue. Caveat: If community-service volunteers need to work in areas where horses are housed, be sure to first move the horses so as to keep your volunteers safe.

Girl Scout troops. Here's another great opportunity for your rescue. Girl Scouts may be able to earn badges in horsemanship or community service by helping with your horses—and with the proper setup you can help them achieve their goals. They can learn how to groom horses, clean out pens, or help run a fund-raiser to benefit the rescue. You'll be teaching the girls about horses, as well as about compassion and responsibility for others.

Join forces with other nonprofit organizations. Consider networking with dog and cat rescues so you'll have someone to contact if you perform a seizure where dogs or cats are involved. You may also find new adopters, foster homes, or volunteers within these rescues. While networking with small-animal rescues, we've been able to help them find adoptive homes for their cats and dogs, and they've assisted us during seizures, and helped to promote our organization.

Therapy programs. By networking with therapy programs that use horses, the purposes of both programs can be furthered. The rescues I've worked with have cooperated with several therapy programs. Our relationships with them have enabled us to serve the community by helping to provide therapy horses for disabled children and adults. This is a win-win situation for the programs and the horses.

The Cedar Ridge Charter School in Lometa, Texas, provides education to children from preschool through high-school seniors. Many of the children who attend come from troubled pasts. They, like the rescue horses we save, were unwanted, abandoned, abused, or neglected. The director of the school, Robin Beauregard, knew about the healing power of horses, so she brought her two geldings to the school for the children to take care of and handle. They were such a big success that Robin decided the school needed its own horses. She contacted the rescue and became a member. Within months, the school had begun fostering horses for the rescue.

Since the children didn't ride, the school offered to foster unridable horses that would enjoy the children's attention. The horses helped the children learn compassion and love, something lacking from so many of their lives. One year after they began fostering, the school adopted four of their foster horses. All of them were older and no longer ridable–not easy horses to place. Although they haven't adopted any more horses, the school now works with the rescue by conducting foster- and adoptive-home inspections, as well as follow-ups.

When I was with Lone Star, we worked with the HELP Center outside of Austin, Texas. The HELP Center offers therapeutic riding sessions to children with a variety of disabilities. The volunteers of the HELP Center began working with rescues when one volunteer adopted a horse named Maple Sugar, who quickly became a favorite therapy horse. The Lone Star volunteer who conducted the pre-adoption inspection was so taken with the program that she began volunteering for it, and before long the two groups shared several volunteers.

The HELP Center began fostering and later adopted two more horses for its program. The riders and their families taught the fostered horses about love and kindness, and sometimes the horses were used for lessons. The two organizations attended events together to raise awareness for both programs. The relationship between the two organizations gave Lone Star a wonderful foster home and a terrific opportunity to help improve the lives of disabled children.

Outreach programs. A perfect example is Creekside Farm Horse Rescue in northeast Texas, which takes its horses to visit local school children. While the horses have been restored to health by the time they visit schools, Creekside President Judith Homer tells the children about the abuse or neglect the horses have suffered. The kids get to pet the horses and ask Judith questions. Many ask why someone wouldn't care for their horse; others ask about what will happen to the horses now that they're healthy; and some just stand by the horse, happy to be able to touch a soft muzzle. Some of the kids have never had a chance to meet a real horse, and Judith hopes these experiences will teach them about love and compassion for all living things. She also hopes that some of the students will grow up to become the rescuers of the future.

If you have miniature horses or donkeys, or small ponies in your rescue, you can develop programs with local nursing homes, hospices, or hospitals. To do this, you'll need to take the time to teach one of your small animals to accept people in wheelchairs and those with crutches or walkers. The animal will need to learn to walk inside buildings, and will need to be desensitized to sudden movements and strange sounds.

Creekside takes its miniature horse, Scrabble Dabble, to visit nursing homes. The residents enjoy the chance to pet a horse (regardless of size), and they often share stories about horse experiences they had while growing up. Organizations that develop nursing-home outreach programs report that the residents are often much more animated and willing to talk when the miniature horses or donkeys come to visit. Some residents, who are normally withdrawn, will come out of their rooms to talk to an equine visitor. As a result, the relatives of the residents often donate money to the rescue or volunteer to help make these programs possible for more people.

Several other rescues have developed programs to work with juvenile offenders and prison inmates. Rescues that work with inmates place horses that need rehabilitation or retraining at prison farms. The inmates work the horses until they're ready to be placed in permanent, adoptive homes.

Programs that work with juvenile offenders invite the youth to their facility to help clean pens, build fences, or work with the horses. Often, both the juvenile offenders and inmates form bonds with the horses they help rehabilitate. For some of them, those bonds are the first they've ever developed with another living being.

The Thoroughbred Retirement Foundation works with prisons in New York, Kentucky, and several other states. The inmates care for the Thoroughbreds at prison farms. Often the horses arrive in desperate need of care, suffering from broken bones, pulled or strained ligaments and tendons, and occasionally from abuse. The prisoners are taught to care for the horses, and as they nurse them back to health, they learn skills they can put to use when they're released from prison. Several inmates have decided to pursue careers in the horse industry upon their release.

As you can see, developing programs with schools, nursing homes, therapy centers, and other similar institutions provides a valuable service to your community and benefits the rescue at the same time. You'll be making a difference in the lives of people of all ages in your community, and while you're earning the community's goodwill, you'll probably pick up a few new donors and volunteers, too.

Educational programs. Providing educational programs, such as riding-lesson programs or summer camps, gives your rescue another way to interact with your community. You can teach children about riding and horse care using well-trained rescue horses. You can also use injured or starving horses to teach the children about rehabilitation, and what happens when people don't provide care for their animals. While doing so, you'll also be teaching them about rescue and cultivating compassion and caring. At the same time, you'll be developing good, educated horse owners of the future.

Another type of educational program is a course to educate new horse owners, or people who're interested in horses but have no hands-on experience. Bluebonnet will soon begin offering such a class throughout Texas and Arkansas. The class will cover such topics as feeding your horse, including appropriate types of feeds and body condition, routine veterinary work and how to identify a veterinary emergency, farrier work, and equine hygiene. Our goal is to educate new horse owners in order to prevent neglect through ignorance, and to generate better-educated horse owners. We'll also discuss the rescue during the class in hopes of recruiting new volunteers and adopters.

During the process of developing these types of programs, you're reaching out to members of your community who may not be active in the horse industry, or may not even own horses. By teaching these people about horses and the need for rescue, you're not only helping to instill compassion in them, but also building a solid foundation for the future. When your organization has a crisis, such as a large seizure, or a horse that requires an expensive surgery, you'll be able to call on your community for assistance.

Your organization is also a member of a larger community–the horse industry, which is composed of many groups that offer networking opportunities. These include: breed registries and associations, riding clubs and associations; 4-H and FFA groups; university and college equine programs; veterinary associations and schools; and equine professional associations, such as the American Association of Equine Practitioners, American Horse Council, and American Farrier's Association.

Remember that networking is a two-way street. When approaching any of these groups for their support, be prepared to offer something of benefit to them. In my experience, it's best to start by approaching local clubs and organizations, as well as the local chapter of national organizations. You might ask these groups if they'd let you have an information booth at upcoming events, or run an ad for your organization in their newsletter. In return, you can offer to list their information on your Web site, help recruit volunteers to work their events, and/or run ads for their organization in your rescue's newsletter.

Local horse clubs often provide enormous support to rescue organizations. Some of these groups might even hold benefits for the rescue, or make donations to it after they get to know your group. Additionally, once the local clubs become familiar with your rescue, they may introduce you to people in national registries and associations who would be willing to network with you.

For example, before I founded Lone Star, I was a member of the Brazos Arabian Horse Association (BAHA), a local Arabian club in Bryan/College Station, Texas. Then when the rescue came along, the Arab club quickly became a great supporter. The rescue ran the concession stand at several BAHA shows with all of the proceeds going to the rescue. We also had a raffle at one BAHA horse show, and were allowed to show off several rescue horses during the lunch break. The Central Texas Arabian Horse Association listed the Arabians we had available for adoption in its newsletter, and a local dressage club put on a used-tack sale to benefit the rescue at one of its events. And recently, The Heart of Texas Morgan Horse Club stepped up to support Bluebonnet, offering us booth space at its events. In exchange for all these benefits, we provide links to the various groups on our Web site and help advertise their events.

Your Community is Your Greatest Asset

To make your networking plans work, you must make community awareness a priority. Have an open house so community members can visit your facilities, meet the rescue horses, and get to know some of the volunteers. Go to community events and meetings to introduce your rescue and let those in attendance know why you exist and how they can help. Approach community groups and offer your organization's support and help with their events. Through these actions you'll open the door for networking within your community. The results will be twofold: Your group will receive aid in achieving its goals, and you'll help the groups with which you network to achieve theirs.

Pepper

"She's just old. Old horses get skinny." That's something we hear far too often when a neglect case involves a skinny horse who is over twenty years old. Pepper was definitely skinny when we first saw her, and she was close to twenty-five years old, but from experience we knew she did not have to be skinny.

Older horses often require a lot more food to help them gain and maintain their weight, and since Pepper was missing several teeth her foster "mom" served her food wet. Day after day, Pepper lapped up her soggy mash and she gained weight—but it was slow. After about a year in the rescue, Pepper looked good but then another problem crept up: She would not shed her long hair, she developed a cresty neck and she grew tender on her front feet. A veterinarian determined that Pepper had Cushing's disease, and her foster home began administering medication.

A few months after she began treatment for Cushing's, Pepper once again looked and felt great. She moved without pain, and she found a home as a beloved pet and companion. Pepper is one of the lucky ones—too many old horses stay skinny and don't get the care they need and deserve.

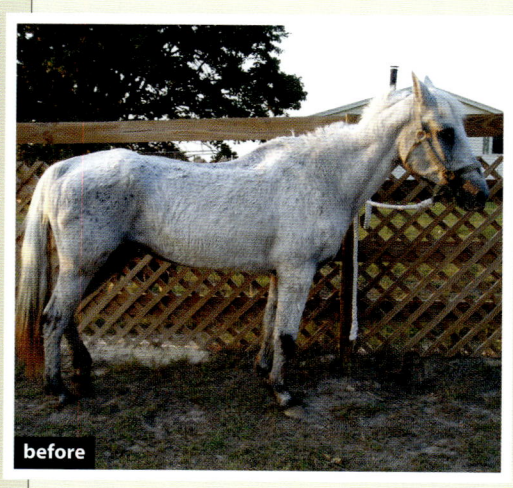

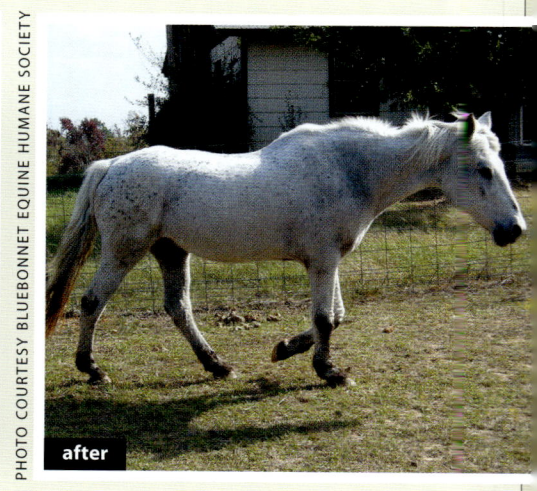

before

after

eleven

Keep Detailed Records

Spend the time up front to set up an efficient record-keeping system.

If you're like me, the last thing you ever wanted to do when you got into rescue was paperwork. Unfortunately, good record-keeping is essential if you want to operate a well-respected, well-run rescue. You'll need to provide accurate records when you're audited, and you'll need them to track where your horses came from and where they're currently located. As part of an audit, or is this a separate issue? Both. Tracking where the horses came from, are currently located, and go is very important so the rescue doesn't "lose" a horse. But any good auditor is going to want to see this kind of record, too. In addition to this, good records make routine veterinary care easy by providing information on when the rescue's horses were last vaccinated, had a Coggins drawn, and had their teeth floated. Well-kept records will enable you to compile the statistics necessary to help secure grants, and can be provided to potential donors upon request.

11 | Keep Detailed Records

There are many aspects of your rescue that must be tracked, and we're going to take a look at all of them.

Corporate Records

The rescue's corporate records are the easiest to assemble. They should be kept at your rescue's office, as listed with the IRS and your state office (often the secretary of state). Per the IRS, if you are a 501(c)(3) you must make these records available to anyone who wishes to examine them. You can do this by scanning corporate documents and posting them on your Web site, by allowing people to inspect the records at your office, or by mailing out copies. Your corporate records include:

Articles of Incorporation. These must be signed by all the incorporators and stamped or approved by the appropriate state office (e.g., the secretary of state in many states).

Determination letter from the IRS. The IRS will issue a letter to you stating that it has granted your organization either provisional or permanent 501(c)(3) status.

Completed 990 forms. Every year you should complete and submit a Form 990 to the IRS. This form shows how much money came into your organization and how much you spent for the year. *Note:* If the organization normally has less than $25,000 in gross receipts in a year, it is not required to file a Form 990. However it is always good to file a Form 990, regardless of whether or not your organization is required to by law—it helps show potential donors that you are a legitimate organization.

Copies of meeting minutes. If your organization has meetings, the minutes of those meetings are part of your corporate records.

Financial Records

Maintaining accurate financial records is essential for a professional organization. As mentioned, you'll need to file a Form 990 with the IRS annually, and accurate financial records are also necessary for audits, when writing grants, and when soliciting donations. Because financial records are so important, some organizations hire a professional bookkeeper. The cost for these services will vary depending on the amount of work required, but this may be a necessary investment if your rescue doesn't have someone with bookkeeping experience who's willing to donate his or her time.

Your financial records begin with an accurate log of all donations that are received by your rescue. You'll use this log to ensure that receipts are sent out for donations, to compile a list of donors to send updates or additional pleas for assistance to, and to report activity to the IRS. Your log should contain the following information on each donation: Donor's full name and address; what was donated (a horse, equipment, money); amount (if monetary); value of material donations (horses, equipment, etc.).

You also need to carefully record all monies coming into the organization, as well as the monies spent. If you or a volunteer will be doing the bookkeeping, consider purchasing a good bookkeeping program. There are several available, and some of them even offer options for nonprofit organizations. You'll find accurate bookkeeping is essential when dealing with the following tasks:

- *Grant-writing.* Organizations that award grants will require an accurate accounting of how you spent their money.
- *IRS reports.* As mentioned, you'll need to file a Form 990 annually, and to do so you'll need an accurate accounting of donations and other income received.
- *State tax reports.* In many states, you'll be required to pay sales tax on anything you sell.

Membership Roster

If your organization offers memberships, you'll need an organized way to track them. Always keep a paper copy of membership forms as a backup for your computer records, even if this means printing out those that are e-mailed to you. However, maintaining a log on your computer is the easiest way to handle your membership roster. You can develop a database using software designed for this purpose, or you can use a spreadsheet to keep track of members. Both ways will allow you to customize the information that you enter, to organize your records by various criteria (such as date), and to search for members. You can use the same methods to keep track of your volunteers.

Horse Records

The records for all your horses must also be complete. They should include information on where each horse came from and where he's currently located, as well as all farrier visits and detailed health reports. Accurate veterinary records for each horse should include:

- A copy of current Coggins test
- Dates of vaccinations, and those given
- Dates of all dental work
- Dates of deworming, and type of product used
- Dates for any additional diagnostics, blood work, or other examinations, and a detailed description of what was done
- Date and cause of death.

Bluebonnet maintains a computer spreadsheet that contains information on each horse, and we also print out a hard copy whenever any of this information is updated. We also include a photograph of each horse, taken of his right and left sides, and front and rear. If a horse has any special conditions when he comes into the rescue, such as extremely overgrown hooves, we also document it with photographs.

Bluebonnet maintains adoption records that include the following information:

- *Adoption application*
- *Reference letters*
- *Pre-adoption inspection report*
- *Adoption contract*
- *Post-adoption inspection follow-ups*
- *Final adoption contract and veterinary report (filled out and submitted two years post-adoption)*
- *Relinquishment paperwork, if an adopted equine is returned.*

Adoption paperwork documents where your horses go once adopted. In the event that someone questions the care that your adopters provide, your records will demonstrate the screening that's done before adopters are approved, and will include the follow-up reports that are made to check up on the care given to horses in their adoptive homes.

These extensive records may seem overwhelming, but they can help save your rescue if you're ever questioned. I've worked with several rescues that have had to rely on their records to prove their actions. In fact, not long after I became involved in rescue, a woman who had donated a horse decided she wanted him back. She insisted the horse still belonged to her, although the rescue had cared for him for several months. However, because our records were complete, we could provide her with a copy of the donation contract she had signed. It stated that she gave up all rights to the horse and transferred ownership to the rescue.

In another incident, a donor insisted that she had the right to visit the horse she'd placed with us. However, we sent her a copy of the donation contract with her signature. The contract clearly stated that she agreed to give up all rights to the horse, including the right to visit.

On another occasion, we were contacted by an animal shelter that had

11 | Keep Detailed Records

just been awarded two horses in a neglect case. When the authorities removed the two horses from their home, they found a third that had died. In court, the owner claimed the horses belonged to the rescue. The director of the animal shelter called to inquire why we would adopt out horses to someone who would let them starve, and why we hadn't checked on them. However, our records showed that although the owner had previously fostered horses for us and had adopted one horse, she had returned the adopted horse over a year before this incident and had not fostered any horses for almost a year and a half. We offered copies of the inspection reports to the animal shelter to demonstrate that when our horses were with her, they were well cared for. This preserved our relationship with the animal shelter and proved that the owner lied in court.

Record-Keeping Systems

How you set up your record-keeping system determines how much time you'll spend managing it. Keeping organized copies of all paperwork enables you to find information when you need it. Even though an electronic database is easier to search, hard copies will provide backup in the event your database is damaged or lost due to equipment failure. For an organization such as Bluebonnet—with officers who are located in various states, and who don't maintain a physical office or facility—an electronic database allows us to easily share information with officers, directors, and staff members.

You have a few options with electronic databases. Spreadsheet programs are one of the easiest ways to maintain electronic records. These programs allow you to decide what information to record, such as name, address, and phone number. Most will allow you to sort the data in ascending or descending order so you can arrange the records in alphabetical order or into a chronological list. For example, you could arrange your membership list by date so you can easily identify which memberships expire in a certain time period.

Electronic databases also provide more sophisticated data-management options and allow more flexibility. You can cross-reference records, so when you look at a member's record, it also tells you that she's approved to foster, and allows you to access a list of the horses she's fostered in the past. Or, when you read a particular horse's record, you can also access information on his current and previous foster homes. Some electronic databases will also enable you to search for items based on multiple criteria. For example, you could search for all horses of a specific breed that were donated during a specific time period.

Databases give you a lot more options, but they're also more difficult to set up. You may need to pay a database designer to create one that meets all your needs.

Another option to consider is an online electronic database. Unfortunately, designing this type of database takes a good deal of programming skills. If you can't find someone willing to donate his time, you could spend anywhere from several hundred to several thousand dollars for a professional programmer to design and implement an online database. However, this type of system will allow your officers, directors, and other key volunteers to access and update database information instantly.

While I was with one rescue, we had an online database designed for us. It was created to meet our unique needs at the time, but several features could be used by multiple rescues. This database could be used and updated by all our officers, and it reduced redundancy in record keeping. Here's a partial list of the features our database offered:

- *A complete list of equine records.* This included the date each horse came into the rescue, where he came from, as well as all his vaccinations, farrier visits, deworming, and other veterinary records. The database also had a section where the user could enter in "from" and "to" dates to generate a list of horses that were due for vaccinations or Coggins within the specified dates.

- *A complete list of membership records.* This included all membership information, as well as a screen where the user could enter "from" and "to" dates to generate a list of members whose memberships would expire during the specified time, and then print out membership renewal notices.

■ *Donor records.* This included such information as name, address, date, and a description of the donation. When the user entered a "from" and "to" date, the database compiled a list of donations received during that time period and printed out receipts.

The database was also designed so that mailing labels could be printed out for those specific members. This makes sending out renewals, donation receipts, and other information quick and easy.

And over time, your database will evolve and include other capabilities that will help your organization run more smoothly.

Back Up Your Records

Regardless of the type of records you keep, you'll need to maintain backup copies of all of it. Keeping electronic records allows for easy backup. You can maintain the hard copies of all applications and paperwork as backup, plus you can back up most databases or spreadsheets on CDs or disks. Sometimes online databases are harder to back up onto CDs, but the ISP (Internet Service Provider) that hosts your database may maintain backups of everything on its servers. You'll need to check with your ISP.

At this point, recording-keeping may seem like a huge hassle, but taking a few minutes each day to stay current can help prevent problems for your organization in the long run. The most difficult part of record-keeping often is deciding how to keep your records and how to set up the system.

Dixie

Over the 4th of July weekend, the rescue received a call from a sheriff's deputy asking for our assistance in investigating a complaint about two starving horses and two starving ponies. When the sheriff's department calls we always jump, so within a few hours one of our investigators visited the horses and the owner along with the deputy. She found one fat pony, one thin pony and two very neglected horses. The owner agreed that she could not feed the horses, but she was very attached to the ponies and did not want to give them up. After speaking to the investigator about what she could do, the owner surrendered the two horses. The investigator warned the owner that she would be back to check on the ponies, loaded up the horses and headed home.

Dixie settled into the foster home's routine quickly and gained weight. As Dixie got stronger, the foster home discovered that she was a pushy horse who seemed to have no ground manners so Dixie's foster

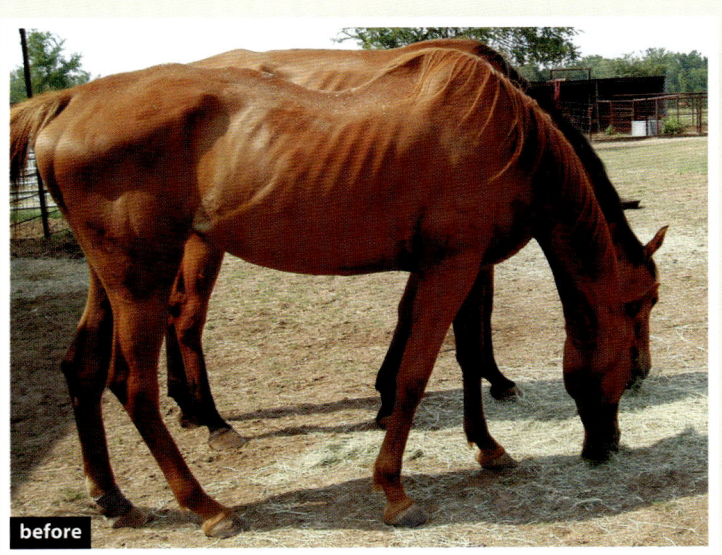

before

PHOTO BY SHARON MARTIN-HOLM

"mom" spent several weeks performing ground work and teaching Dixie to respect her and not walk over her. Once she was healthy and respectful, her foster owner also evaluated her under saddle. Although Dixie had a sway-back, it didn't seem to bother her under saddle—but it was hard to find a saddle with enough padding to fit her comfortably!

Today Dixie is healthy, sleek, and happy—and a nice riding horse. She's still looking for her "forever home," but I have no doubt that she'll find one soon.

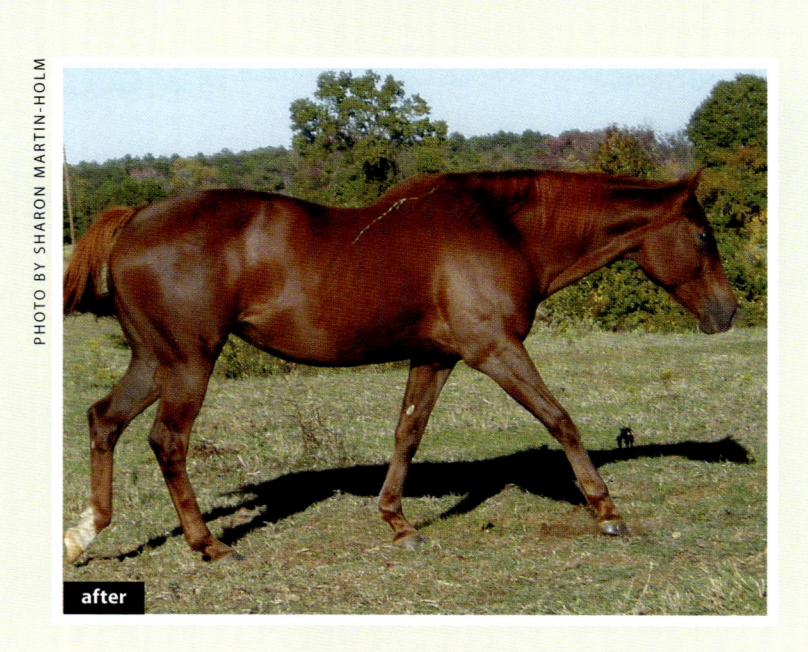

PHOTO BY SHARON MARTIN-HOLM

after

twelve

Insurance

Without insurance, you can lose everything in the blink of an eye.

When I surveyed rescues across the country, I was amazed to learn that very few of them have insurance. Many of these groups say they haven't even thought about getting insurance, and others say it just hasn't been a priority for them. I've even been told that insurance isn't really necessary because nothing could happen that would warrant the expense. Yikes.

As we all know (or should), accidents can happen even when you're careful to take necessary precautions. You could be held liable in a wide range of circumstances, and it could cost your organization a great deal of money if you don't have insurance. Consider the following:

- A volunteer at your facility is leading a horse into the pasture when another horse spins around and kicks her, breaking her arm.
- You're working with law-enforcement agents, and a horse is injured

during the seizure. The horse is later returned to his owner, but the injury has rendered him unridable.
- A horse you've taken to a pet event bites a child. The child must be rushed off to the hospital where he requires stitches.
- A horse gets loose at a horse show or clinic you've put on as a fundraiser. Before he can be caught, he runs into another horse, causing him to spook and throw his rider. The rider is badly hurt and taken to a local hospital.
- A fire starts at your rescue facility, completely destroying your tackroom. You lose halters, lead ropes, saddles, bridles, and all sorts of other training and riding equipment.

The above scenarios are only a few of the possible situations your rescue could face. The people involved in these or similar circumstances could decide to sue your organization for medical costs, veterinary bills, and more. Without insurance, such lawsuits could bankrupt your rescue. So, let's take a look at the different types of insurance you might consider appropriate for your organization.

Property Insurance

This provides coverage for the property owned by your organization. The specific events or perils that your property is covered against will be listed in your policy, and may include fire, tornadoes, or theft. Some policies also cover flood damage, but this type of protection often requires a separate policy. Equipment housed on the property or in any of its structures may be covered, but you'll need to review the specifics of any policy you're considering to ensure that you're getting complete coverage. Some examples of situations that might be covered by property insurance include:
- Someone breaks into the rescue's barn and steals all your tack. Your policy may cover the cost of replacing it.

- A lightning strike sparks a fire that burns your feed shed. Your insurance may cover the cost to replace the shed and its contents.

Liability Insurance

This provides coverage for bodily injury and property damage (to others) for which the rescue may be held liable. Again, you'll have to work out with your agent the specifics of what's covered under your rescue's policy. Here are some of the situations which liability insurance might cover:

- A prospective donor (or adopter) visits your facility and is bitten by a horse. She sues your rescue for her medical bills.
- A prospective adopter visits one of your horses at his foster home. While test-riding him, she's thrown off, breaks her leg, and is off work for a week. She sues your organization for medical bills and loss of income.
- Someone attends one of your fund-raisers, and while there he's injured by a loose horse, suffering a concussion and several broken bones. He sues your organization for medical bills and loss of income.
- One of your horses escapes from your facility or a foster home, gets onto a roadway, and causes an accident. Those involved in the accident sue you for medical costs and damage to their vehicles.

Again, it's important to remember that accidents can happen at any time. Medical bills for people injured by one of your horses can be expensive, and a lawsuit could easily bankrupt your rescue. Liability insurance offers your group invaluable protection.

D&O (Directors and Officers) Insurance

The directors and officers of nonprofit organizations may be targeted by lawsuits alleging abuse of authority, mismanagement of funds, and more. D&O insurance is designed to protect your organization and its individual officers and directors from liabilities that may result from the performance of their assigned tasks. It also protects any covered individual or group (such as the board of directors) against "wrongful act" lawsuits. These are generally defined as the actual or perceived breach of duty, neglect, misstatement, omission, misleading statement, or error performed during the discharge of an individual or group's duties (providing the individual or group is covered under your D&O policy) while acting in their capacity with your organization. D&O insurance can also cover your organization against lawsuits alleging failure to manage and supervise the activities of the rescue. And finally, this type of insurance can also offer some protection to volunteers and staff members who are engaging in activities under your supervision.

As with all insurance policies, the specific officer, director, staff, and/or volunteer positions, and the types and amounts of claims covered should be specified in your individual policy. Here are some of the situations that may be covered in a D&O policy:

- Your BOD votes to remove a member who has broken the rules. The member then sues the directors because her removal from the board has deprived her of her rights as a member. She claims the directors "abused their authority."
- One of your donors is angry that you spent money to purchase a horse at auction and then euthanized him because your organization couldn't afford the expensive surgery he needed to live comfortably. The donor charges that you should have spent the money to save a "healthier" horse, and sues the directors for "mismanagement of funds."
- Your organization works with local law-enforcement officers to execute a seizure of starving horses. In court, your volunteers present evidence demonstrating neglect of the horses. The owner sues the volunteers for defamation of character.

Vehicle Insurance

This type of insurance isn't optional. If your organization owns any vehicles, you'll need to provide proof of insurance to register them. Your organization needs a policy that covers each vehicle it owns. Also, make sure that any volunteers who'll be driving these vehicles have their own insurance, and that any trailers being towed by those vehicles are covered in your policy.

If your volunteers will be using their own vehicles while doing business for your rescue, you'll also need "non-owned" vehicle insurance. If one of your volunteers gets into an accident while trailering one of your horses, or is simply driving somewhere on rescue business, you could be sued for medical bills or the cost of repairs to the other person's vehicle. Non-owned automobile insurance will provide coverage for your group should this happen.

Workers Compensation Insurance

Laws vary from state to state, but rescues that have employees may also need workers compensation insurance. This type of coverage will help protect your organization from lawsuits filed by employees who are injured while working for the rescue. Here are some of the situations in which this type of insurance would provide protection:

- An employee is thrown from a horse, breaking his leg. Workers compensation may pay for his medical bills.
- Another employee is seriously injured while trying to load a horse during a seizure. She's not only hospitalized, but also unable to work for two months. Workers compensation may cover her medical bills and lost wages.
- An employee is killed in an automobile accident while trailering horses to your facility. Workers compensation may provide "death benefits" to his two children.

You'll need to check your own state's laws to determine whether or not you need to purchase workers compensation insurance and how it's regulated in your state.

Care, Custody, and Control

If your group will be working with law enforcement to seize horses from neglectful homes, and plans to take responsibility for housing them at the group's facility or in foster homes, ask your agent about insurance for "care, custody, and control." This type of coverage will protect your organization in the event a horse you're temporarily holding for any law-enforcement agency is injured or killed while in your care. Since you don't own the horse, his owner could sue your organization for the horse's value, or even for the emotional distress associated with his loss. This may be covered under your general liability policy, but it often requires separate coverage or a rider to your original liability policy. Check with your agent for specifics on care, custody, and control. *Note:* Bluebonnet's policy only covers us for a specific number of horses, and we'll have to increase this number—along with the cost of our insurance—as we take in more horses.

Don't Leave Home Without It

Because rescues have unique needs, they often have difficulty finding an insurance carrier that can meet their requirements. This is especially true for rescues that run foster-home programs. While some organizations need property and/or liability insurance to cover events they hold at their facility, or the people who visit, they also need coverage when taking their horses to public events, holding fund-raisers, and placing horses in adoptive homes. Because of the risks involved in these circumstances, it can take many months to find insurance.

When I researched insurance for the first rescue I was involved with, it took over two years to locate an insurance agent willing to write a policy that would provide the coverage we needed. If you end up struggling to find insurance, be patient. Ask other rescue groups who provides their coverage, and keep talking to insurers. This is too important an issue for you to give up.

When you meet with potential insurance agents, be prepared to provide information on your organization, and to describe how it runs. Following is a list of details you'll need to provide to help an agent devise a policy to suit your rescue's needs:

- Size of your facility, and the average number of horses housed there at any time
- Number of foster homes in your network
- Number of horses in your rescue at any time (in foster care or housed at a facility)
- Number of members
- Number of volunteers
- Number of fund-raisers you plan per year
- Descriptions of any programs offered by your organization
- Description of any additional activities your rescue engages in
- Copies of adoption and fostering policies and contracts.

All of this information will help the agent put together the best possible coverage for your organization. If the agent you're working with can develop insurance policies to suit your needs, ask for a copy of each proposed policy and schedule another meeting to discuss them. Give yourself plenty of time to carefully read over each policy, and be sure to ask the agent about any questions you have during your next meeting. If there's anything you're uncomfortable with or that you feel has been left out, you need to discuss it with your agent before you sign the policy or pay the company. Also, make sure you clearly understand the process for filing claims.

12 | Insurance

Once your insurance policy is finalized and signed, keep several copies on hand. It's also wise to have a copy of the procedure for handling claims on hand. If you have vehicle insurance, keep a copy of the claims procedure in each vehicle, and keep another copy in your office. If any of your rescue's information changes—the number of horses you're housing, the number of volunteers, or anything else—you need to notify your insurance agent immediately.

When you're planning fund-raisers or other public events, you should also check with your agent to make sure they'll be covered. And always be careful to adhere to the terms of your insurance policy. If you fail to do so, your insurance may be cancelled or claims may not be covered.

Insurance for rescue organizations can be expensive. You may pay as little as $2,000 per year, or as much as $25,000 per year depending on the type of insurance you need, your deductibles, the number of horses your organization houses, and the number and types of events you have planned.

Your insurance may also limit the types of activities you can engage in. For instance, you may not be able to hold trail rides for fund-raisers, or to do photo shoots with your horses. However, the protection provided by insurance far outweighs the expense and limitations. I strongly urge you to secure insurance for your rescue organization before you begin working with the public.

Tucker

When Tucker came to the rescue, we were still accepting "donated" horses from people who could no longer care for them. (Later that year we stopped accepting donated horses and only took in neglect cases.) His owner had purchased him for her seven-year-old daughter. Although Tucker was very skinny when he arrived at their home, the child immediately began riding him. The family could not put or keep weight on him, so they decided to rehome him and hoped that the rescue could help him gain weight and then find him a home.

When Tucker's new foster "mom" first saw him, she could not believe that someone had been riding him. He was so thin that carrying a saddle and rider must have been painful for him. She vowed to help him gain weight before anyone else rode him. Since Tucker was a big, older horse, he needed a lot of food each meal to help him keep his weight—and it was not cheap

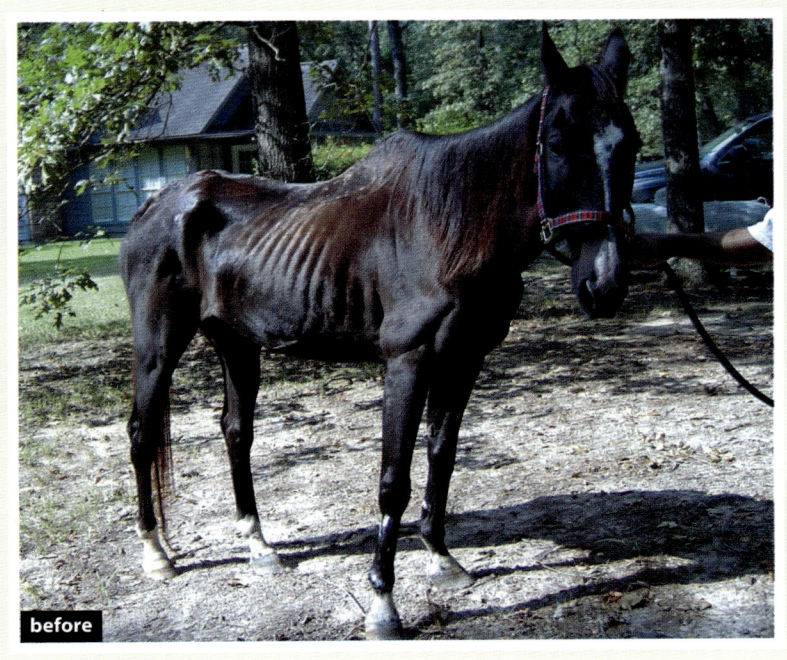

before

PHOTO BY MARIANNE SKARPA

to feed him! To make matters worse, Tucker was a sensitive horse: he did not like being separated from other horses and would stop eating if he couldn't see his equine companions.

Although it wasn't easy, six months after he arrived Tucker was once again healthy and the rescue began a quest to find the perfect home. He was well-broke to ride, but he was 25 years old and deserved to take things easy. And while he wasn't eating as much as he had when he was gaining weight, he still required two big meals each day, which included grain as well as soaked beet pulp. While we searched for that perfect home for this old gentleman, his foster "mom" realized that she had come to love him too much to let him go and decided to adopt him. They now take short, leisurely rides together and Tucker has a safe, loving home and plenty of food for the rest of his life.

PHOTO BY JODI LUECKE

after

thirteen

How to Battle Burnout

The demands of rescue work make burnout a major threat to the work force.

As I sit down to write this chapter, I'm suffering from burnout. I've been putting in too many hours and taking too little time off. The stress of organizing horse seizures, worrying about finances, and thinking about the horses we couldn't save has caught up with me. I'm worn out. Once burnout sets in, I don't want anything to do with the rescue–even reading e-mail seems a chore. But I've been burned out before, so I know the feeling will pass, and once it does I'll feel re-energized and ready to tackle new projects.

What exactly is burnout? According to Webster, it's emotional stress from responsibilities, but to me it's more than that—it's also mental and physical exhaustion caused by a long-term, excessively passionate devotion to a cause. The condition can be exaggerated when you also feel disillusioned about the cause you're working for, or you overextend yourself. When this occurs, you lose all motivation for the job you were doing—whether you're an employee, a volunteer, or the head of an organization.

TELLTALE SIGNS OF BURNOUT

Some people will exhibit several signs of burnout before they experience it, while others may experience it with few symptoms. Here's what to look for:

- **fatigue**
- **recurring illness**
- **problems sleeping**
- **cynicism, toward either the people in the rescue, or the people/situations your rescue encounters**
- **feelings of helplessness**
- **frustration**
- **unreasonable anger against those believed to be responsible for a certain situation (for example, thinking or saying things like, "I'd just like to beat the snot out of the guy who starved his horse")**
- **depression**
- **isolating yourself from friends and/or family**
- **detachment from the organization (for example, sudden withdrawal or isolation from rescue friends, ceasing to volunteer, not fulfilling commitments to the organization, and avoiding the group's social events and other functions)**
- **harshness when dealing with others, either other volunteers or members of the public**
- **anxiety, either about specific rescue problems or generalized feelings of anxiety**
- **physical pain in your body**
- **change in eating patterns**
- **increased smoking, drinking, or use of drugs**
- **general irritability**
- **reluctance to go to work (volunteer or paid)**
- **difficulty making decisions.**

Rescue work is physically, emotionally, and mentally demanding, so burnout is a common occurrence. However, some people don't recover and end up leaving rescue work altogether. When the leader of an organization burns out, the rescue may end up being closed; when volunteers burn out, you can lose foster homes, people to trailer horses, and staff who help keep your organization running smoothly. Obviously, burnout is a big issue in rescue!

Passionate people who are very committed to a cause are the most likely to suffer from burnout. This is important to understand because rescue work naturally attracts this type of person. People in rescue care deeply about the horses they help, and they tend to put all their effort and energy behind the cause. Look at your hardest-working volunteers–they're very passionate about your organization—they spend all their free time working with your horses, promoting your rescue, and going to events for the organization. Their lives are entwined with the rescue and its horses. Unfortunately, the same passion that drives rescuers to accomplish great things can quickly turn to severe burnout.

Another factor that plays a role in burnout is disillusionment. This occurs when you feel the problems are just too big or too difficult to solve. Disillusionment begins when rescuers are overwhelmed with the number of horses that need help. Sometimes it seems there are just too many—thousands go through auctions each week, hundreds wind up in the slaughterhouses, and so many are neglected and abused each day. Rescues have finite resources—there's simply not enough money or time to help every horse, and sometimes this is overwhelming.

Working on neglect cases also causes disillusionment. After removing emaciated horses from deplorable conditions, or taking several complaints of abuse or neglect, it's easy to feel that people are too cruel, the problems are too overwhelming, and you won't be able to make a difference.

Lack of appreciation is another factor that contributes to feelings of disillusionment. For example, let's say you spent weeks working on a grant. You researched the issues, and worked with the granting organization to set it up. But when your organization receives the money, instead of being thanked by the rescue's directors or officers, you're bombarded with complaints. The grant isn't big enough, it's too difficult to administer, or it wasn't for the "right" project. Or, perhaps you've just spent weeks putting together the Web site for your organization. But when it's published to the Internet, members complain about the format or don't think you included enough information. While you don't mind constructive criticism and ideas, you feel unappreciated when it seems that no one remembers to thank you for your work.

But it's not always easy to understand why rescuers feel unappreciated. Consider this: You have a volunteer who believes the rescue should allow her to adopt a horse for free in exchange for her volunteer efforts. But rescue policy doesn't permit this, and when the directors or officers refuse to make an exception, the volunteer resents their decision and becomes disillusioned with the rescue. You don't think her disillusionment is valid—she knew the organization's policies and knew they must be followed.

In another case, a volunteer offers to put on a fund-raiser for your organization. Part of your fund-raising policy requires that event coordinators provide weekly reports to the officers detailing their progress toward the fund-raiser. This particular volunteer refuses to submit reports or to answer questions about the event, so you must replace her with someone able to follow the rescue's policies. She feels unappreciated and tells other volunteers that she's disillusioned with the rescue.

Even if you believe your volunteers' feelings of disillusionment are invalid, those feelings can still lead to burnout. Ensuring that your volunteers read and understand the policies and procedures of your organization may help in some of these cases—that way your volunteers will know what's expected of them up front. If your rescue's policies are long, you might consider creating fact sheets that list the pertinent details. Bluebonnet has a "Fostering Fact Sheet" that lists the requirements for foster homes and what's expected of them. The sheet is in a bulleted format, making it easier for volunteers to read and reference. You can also provide each volunteer with a manual that has a copy of each policy, form, and standard operating procedure.

Who's at Risk?

Understanding the causes and symptoms of burnout, and how to combat it, can help you prevent it and cope with it when it does occur. Those people most at risk for burnout share several characteristics:

- They tend to be the most passionate people in your organization.
- They tend to completely immerse themselves in the rescue's work.
- They may volunteer for multiple responsibilities or positions immediately after they join the rescue.
- They may slowly become involved, but tend to add responsibilities over time until they've taken on more than they can reasonably handle.

Volunteers who are at a high risk for burnout have very high self-expectations. They believe they can do a better job than anyone else, and they're not satisfied with anything less than absolute perfection. Not only do these people have trouble saying "no" when asked to take on more responsibilities, they also have trouble asking others to help them with their responsibilities or admitting when they've taken on too much. Sometimes, these volunteers believe they can do a better job if they keep doing more.

Volunteers who put their rescue work first in their lives—above their regular job, their own animals, and their family—are also candidates for burnout. These people tend to use their vacation time, and may even call in sick to their workplace, in order to do rescue work. They neglect their own families or drag them to rescue events each weekend, forcing them to volunteer. Sometimes, these volunteers may stop training, showing, or riding their own horses in order to spend more time with the rescue. They may abandon their friends and give up all hobbies.

Initially, these seem like great volunteers—after all, they're always willing to reschedule their plans to help the rescue. However, I've known several volunteers who've done this—and none of them are still volunteering with my organization. One such volunteer called in sick so often that her boss became concerned that she was seriously ill. Another volunteer had to quit the rescue when her husband insisted that she stop because she no longer spent time with her children!

You may have no trouble identifying with several of these characteristics because you may possess them yourself, and you'll often find them in your most dedicated volunteers. They're probably the people you can call anytime night or day, because you know you can always count on them. Unfortunately these are the people with the highest risk of burning out. To help your organization keep these dedicated volunteers, you need to understand the signs of burnout (see "Telltale Signs of Burnout," on page 168) and how to prevent it.

Prevention is the Key

Almost every volunteer occasionally exhibits some signs of burnout. As long as the symptoms are temporary and not overwhelming, the volunteer will likely recover quickly. When symptoms linger or become overwhelming, the person suffers from burnout. Obviously drug usage, increased alcohol consumption, and changes in appetite can be physically dangerous, while other symptoms, such as fatigue and depression, can be hazardous to your volunteer's mental health. Preventing burnout is important and if prevention fails, burnout should be treated quickly.

So how do you prevent burnout in yourself and your volunteers? Be on the lookout for the characteristics of people who are likely to burn out. (See "Who's at Risk?" on page 171.) If you recognize those characteristics in yourself, don't allow yourself to take on too many responsibilities. Set limits—decide how much work you can reasonably handle, and when people ask you to do more, say no. If you are one of the organization's leaders, remember to delegate jobs to other people so you won't become overwhelmed. If you notice another volunteer taking on too much work, talk to her about burnout and limit her responsibilities.

Taking time off from rescue work is also helpful. Take vacation, and leave contact information with the rescue's officers—making it clear that they should only contact you in the event of an emergency. Pick at least one night a week on which you don't do rescue work—instead, go out to a movie and dinner with your friends and family. Time off allows you to recuperate from the stress of rescue. When I take time off, I come back feeling refreshed and ready to attack new projects.

Volunteers with a strong support system often fight off burnout better than those who feel like no one understands or cares about their rescue work. The truth is, your spouse, family, and friends who are not involved in the rescue probably don't understand your passion. However, if they're supportive of the work you do, occasionally volunteering or participating in fund-raisers, you won't feel so alone. Having understanding friends within the rescue, or others who can sympathize and listen to your rescue problems, will also help to alleviate burnout.

Member-appreciation programs can be a great way to help combat burnout since members and volunteers who feel unappreciated for their work are most likely to suffer burnout and leave your group. Organize a volunteer party, member-appreciation trail ride, or a volunteer-awards program. The first year I worked with a rescue, I organized a volunteer trail ride. The rescue purchased burgers and hot dogs, and members brought side dishes. Some members went out riding while others sat around and chatted.

For my last event on behalf of that same horse rescue, I put together a

WAYS TO PREVENT OR OVERCOME BURNOUT

Sometimes we miss the signs that point to impending burnout, or we can tell it's on the way but don't know how to prevent it. Luckily, there are several things you can do to help overcome burnout.

- **Remember what attracted you to the organization in the first place.** Remind yourself how fulfilling your job is, and consider the reasons why. Write a list of the organization's good points, as well as the things about your job that appeal to you, and review it frequently.
- **Consider the specific things about your volunteer job or the organization that make you feel frustrated or disillusioned.** Are the problems as big as you think? What can you do to resolve them?
- **Seek support.** Talk to other volunteers and/or the rescue's officers about your burnout. Ask them to help you cut back on your responsibilities, and ask how they cope with burnout. Talk to friends or family members as well.
- **Set limits.** Decide what you can reasonably handle and learn how to say no when people ask for more than you feel you can give.
- **Cut back on low-priority jobs and responsibilities.** If you feel you've overextended yourself, evaluate what you really want to contribute to the organization, and then cut back on volunteer jobs that don't support your goals.
- **Learn to delegate.** If you're in a position of authority, you can't do everything. Work with trusted volunteers to accomplish specific tasks.
- **Recognize your limitations—and accept them.**
- **Take care of yourself physically and mentally.** Eat well, get plenty of sleep, and remember to exercise. Take time off to hang out with friends and family, or take a vacation. Keep in mind that making time for yourself and relaxation are two of the best ways to fight or prevent burnout.

pizza party and awards ceremony for the volunteers. The rescue purchased pizza and soft drinks, and someone donated a cake. I presented each officer and director with a small gift as a token of appreciation for all their rescue work. We also awarded T-shirts to those members who had been with the rescue for five years, and we gave out awards based on the number of horses fostered while with the rescue.

I also made up some silly awards, such as the "Nursing Home for Senior Equines," which was given to the foster home that had nursed several horses back to health. The "Foster Home Survival Kit" went to the foster home that had fostered the most difficult horses. It included aspirin (for the headaches the horses gave their caretakers), and margarita mix (to help the foster "parent" relax after a difficult day). My husband and I made most of the awards, so the costs for the party were minimal, but everyone had a great time. This event enabled me to tell all of our members how much I appreciated their contributions.

You Can Beat Burnout

When I began writing this chapter, I was feeling burned out and ready to leave the rescue. However, as I researched methods of combating burnout and started to put them to use, I began to feel better. I discussed my feelings with the rescue's directors, and we began working together to improve my job. I also took a mini-vacation with my husband, and I came back feeling energized and ready to jump back into rescue work with renewed passion.

When you're feeling the telltale symptoms of burnout, remember your rescue needs you. More importantly, the animals depend on your help. If you quit, who will help them? When you're tempted to overextend yourself, remember that if you set yourself up for burnout, you can't help any animals. It's better to do a little less right now so you can continue to volunteer for years to come.

Nickers

One hot summer day, our rescue received a call from someone who'd seen a horse that was hundreds of pounds underweight, and she worried that if we didn't act immediately the horse would die. When our volunteer arrived on the scene with a sheriff's deputy, she found a starving, aged horse. She informed the owner that he could voluntarily surrender the horse, and when he refused, the deputy obtained a warrant to forcibly remove the animal.

The first few days were touch and go for Nickers. He was so thin that you could count not only his ribs, but also the vertebrae in his neck and spine. He was weak and lethargic, and we weren't sure he would make it. Nickers slowly gained weight and strength, and by the time his owner was due in court on animal-neglect charges, he looked gorgeous.

Nickers' gentle personality and kind attitude won over his caretakers. When it was time for Nickers to go up for adoption, his foster dad couldn't stand the thought of parting with him. So Nickers' foster mom adopted him and presented him to her husband as a surprise gift at a Bluebonnet clinic. Nickers' new person was amazed by his wife's gift—and the spectators were touched by Nickers' story.

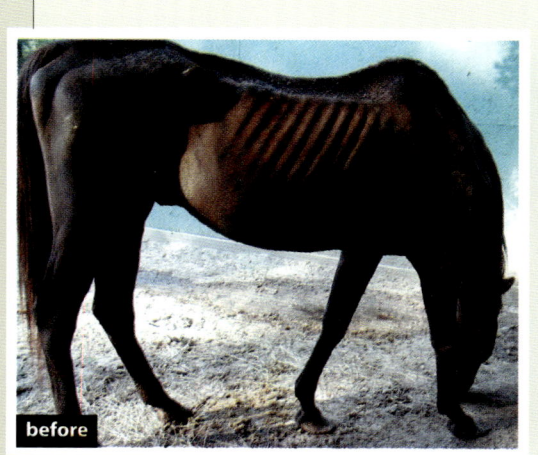

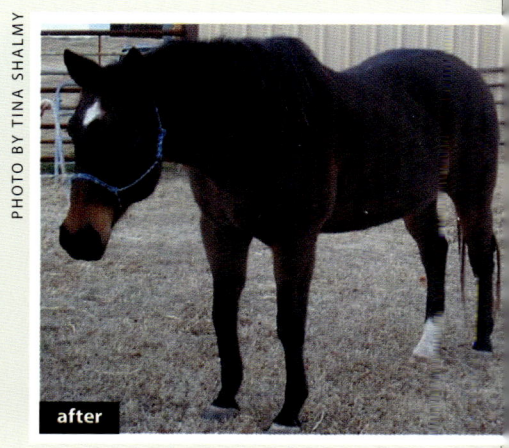

PHOTO BY TINA SHALMY — before

PHOTO BY TINA SHALMY — after

fourteen

How to Assess Body Condition

Learn how to put a horse's condition into quantitative terms that even the courts can understand.

In 1983, Dr. Don Henneke, a graduate student at Texas A&M University, was working on a study of conception rates in mares, depending on body weight. He needed a precise method to gauge the overall physical condition of the mares so they could be divided into classifications, such as "average," "thin," and "overweight." Within the thin and overweight classifications, he further required a system to determine which mares were "slightly" thin or overweight, "moderately" thin or overweight, and those who were emaciated or obese. What he came up with is the Henneke Body Condition (HBC) Scoring Chart, which rates the condition of a horse regardless of breed, age, or sex.

The HBC Scoring Chart is now used throughout the country to objectively describe the condition of horses. Law-enforcement agencies often use HBC scores when obtaining a warrant to seize horses and in court cases to demonstrate neglect. Rescues and humane societies routinely record HBC scores upon an animal's arrival and use them as a baseline to track his progress throughout rehabilitation. Breeding farms, veterinary clinics, and university horse programs also use HBC scores to quantitatively identify the condition of horses upon arrival at their facilities.

At Bluebonnet, we frequently use HBC scores. When a new horse comes into the rescue, we record his body-condition score (BCS). The foster homes of horses that are undergoing rehabilitation submit monthly reports to our horse coordinator that include photographs and updated HBC scores. This allows us to track how much each horse improves from month to month, and to identify those that aren't progressing as quickly as expected.

When one of our volunteers performs a post-adoption or foster follow-up home visit, she assigns a BCS to each horse. For our foster homes, this helps to ensure that they're submitting adequate body-condition scores during their monthly reports. If a horse's condition fails to improve as expected, or his score decreases, our coordinator can discuss the horse's care with the foster home or adopter, or make an appointment to have a veterinarian examine the horse. In the worst cases, a decreasing BCS may indicate that we need to move the horse to a new home.

Our volunteers also use HBC scores when working with law enforcement. During a neglect or abuse investigation, our investigators assign body-condition scores to every horse on the reported property. When HBC scores are low enough to show neglect, we then present that information along with photographs of the animals to law-enforcement officers, and request that the authorities obtain a warrant to seize the horses and any other equines. During an actual seizure, each horse is caught, assigned a case number, photographed, and then given an HBC score before being loaded into a trailer and transported to a holding facility.

In court, HBC scores are presented along with a description of the scoring system to quantifiably demonstrate neglect. Even when judges or jury members lack knowledge about proper horse care, once the scoring system has been explained to them, they can understand that a horse with a low score is underweight and suffering from neglect.

How This System Works

The HBC scoring chart divides a horse's body into six major parts: neck, withers, shoulder, ribs, loins, and tailhead. Each area is rated from a 1 (extremely poor) to 9 (extremely fat or obese). A scoring chart provides a description for each score (1-9), for each area of the horse's body. For example, when the bone structure of a horse's neck is easily visible it earns a BCS of 1; when bulging with fat it scores a 9. Scores are assigned after visual assessment, as well as palpation of the area when possible. (Sometimes it's not possible to palpate wild horses or those that have been severely abused and are unwilling to be touched.) When horses have long hair coats, those assigning body-condition scores must palpate the horses because long hair can obscure a horse's condition. If you can't touch them, you have to visually assess them but know that your scores are likely higher than normal since you cannot touch the horse to see what's underneath the long hair.

Scores for all six areas are totaled and divided by six to give an overall BCS. Horses with a BCS near 1.0 are often referred to as "walking skeletons" because most of their bone structure is easily visible even from a distance. Horses who receive a score of 8 to 9 are obese, with visible bulges and rolls of fat. A BCS of 5.0 is ideal, although scores between 4 and 6 are acceptable. Horses that score over a 7.0 are in danger of health problems, such as laminitis, joint problems, and colic. Racehorses, endurance horses, and others that are involved in demanding disciplines may score around 4.0—they appear very lean but well-muscled. Horses with a BCS under 4.0 are considered neglected, and those with a BCS of 1 to 2 are in critical need of intervention. Courts throughout the United States accept HBC scores as a means of demonstrating neglect and will often remove horses that score below 3.0 from their owners.

While some horse owners claim that mares that are in foal, nursing a foal, or recently weaned a foal, have reason to be in less-than-ideal body condition, the Henneke Body Condition Scoring Chart doesn't make allowances for this. Additionally, many people argue that it's normal for aged horses to be in lower body condition, but HBC scoring doesn't allow for differences by age, either. The fact is that horse owners may simply need to supply aged horses, pregnant mares, and nursing mares with additional food or supplements to help them maintain their weight.

In some cases, there are medical reasons why a horse can't or shouldn't be maintained in a BCS of 5.0. For horses with lameness problems, such as laminitis or severe arthritis, any additional weight could actually complicate their lameness issues. In these cases, a BCS between a 4.0 and 4.5 is better for the horse's comfort. (Since horses naturally carry the majority of their weight on their front end, the heavier a horse is the more weight he'll carry on his front feet. For the horse with front-end lameness this means increased mobility problems and pain.) Veterinary records should document any specific health conditions, but even then a horse shouldn't drop below a score of 4.0.

Of course, there are exceptions to every rule. You may come across a horse with a poor BCS, but when you speak to the owner you learn that he's feeding the horse an appropriate diet, maintains him on a good deworming program, and has routine dental work performed. If the owner isn't already working with his veterinarian to determine the cause of the horse's condition, you can encourage him to invest in a blood-chemistry panel and complete blood count (CBC), as well as an overall veterinary examination. This may help him determine what's wrong with his horse. If the owner and his vet can't determine a reason for the horse's body condition, and the horse seems otherwise happy and free of pain, he's not a candidate to be seized or removed from his owner.

Ensure Proper Training

Since body-condition scoring is an important tool for rescues, your organization needs to provide training to volunteers who will use the HBC scoring chart. Volunteers who have participated in a comprehensive body-condition-scoring training program will make more credible witnesses in court, and will provide your organization with more accurate assessments than those who are inexperienced. Your training program should include three components:

(**1.**) Give each volunteer a printed copy of the Henneke Body Condition Scoring Chart. Include an outline of a horse that indicates each area the volunteer must score. This handout should also include a description of how to score each area of a horse's body. (See "Example of HBC Scoring," on page 183.) A volunteer with experience in assigning body-condition scores or a trainer needs to review the chart with each new volunteer.

(**2.**) An experienced volunteer should then assign body-condition scores to several horses while describing how she determines the scores.

(**3.**) The trainee should then assign body-condition scores to several horses. The trainer, or an experienced volunteer, can discuss any discrepancies in scoring with the volunteer. If the new volunteer's scores are more than 0.25 points different from the trainer's scores, she should continue practicing until her scores match those of the trainer's.

When you put together training classes, invite local animal-control officers, sheriff's deputies, and other law-enforcement officers who investigate reports of neglect. This not only will help educate the officers about scoring the horses they investigate, but also will give you a great opportunity to introduce your rescue and network.

After you've trained some volunteers, consider initiating a policy that one trained volunteer will assign body-condition scores in the following situations:

- When investigating a report of neglect. While the volunteer may not be able to palpate each of the horses, she can visually assess them and assign an approximate BCS.

- When removing horses from neglectful owners. This is especially important when preparing a court case. Each horse should be assigned a BCS before it is moved from the owner's property. Unless the horse is wild and cannot be touched, the volunteers who assign body-condition scores should visually assess the horse as well as palpate each area. Then before going to court, re-evaluate each horse and assign a new BCS. This will demonstrate how the horses have improved while receiving proper care.

- Whenever a new horse comes into your rescue, and at least once every other month while he's in your care. Sometimes it's hard to tell how much weight a horse is gaining when you see him every day. However, if you document his body condition when he enters your rescue, and then record his BCS each month or every other month, you can easily identify changes in condition.

You'll find this method of assessing a horse's condition will become an invaluable tool in your quest to save horses. The use of body-condition scoring will enable you to put neglect into quantitative terms that members of the court can more easily understand.

EXAMPLE OF HBC SCORING

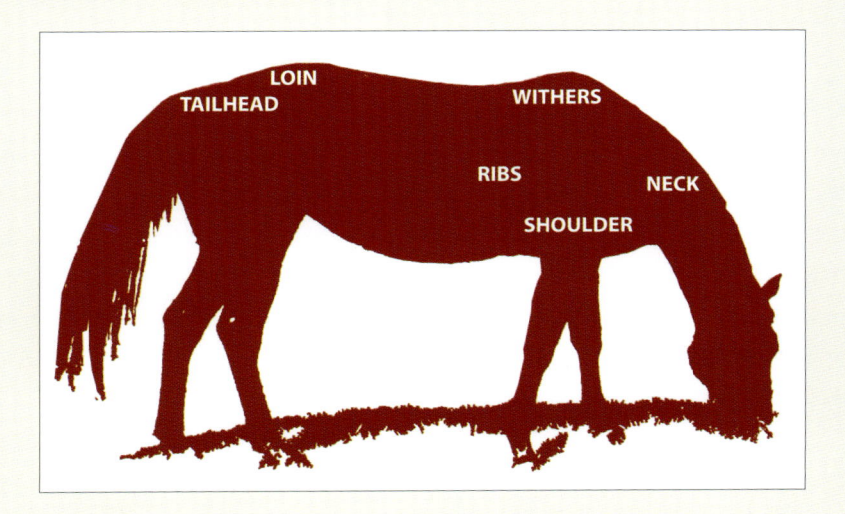

RIBS

Score	Description
1	The ribs project prominently.
2	The ribs are prominent.
3	There is a slight fat covering, but the ribs are still clearly visible.
4	There is a slight fat covering over the ribs, and the ribs are slightly visible.
5	The ribs are not visible, but they can be easily felt.
6	The fat over the ribs feels soft and spongy, but they can still be felt.
7	Individual ribs may be palpated, but there is fat located between each rib.
8	The ribs are difficult to feel.
9	The ribs cannot be felt and there are patches of fat located over the ribs.

Note: You may be able to obtain a copy of the Henneke Body Condition Scoring Chart from your agriculture extension service.

Trooper

Some of the rescue's volunteers were attending an auction to purchase a few horses that would otherwise go to slaughter. As one of the volunteers waited outside with her truck and trailer, ready to drive the newest rescue horses home, one skinny brown horse caught her eye. Although Linda kept trying to look away, the horse had her attention and she knew she had to bring him home. So the rescue ended up buying him before the auction had even begun. As Linda led him towards her waiting horse trailer, several men guffawed at the kindness of the rescue volunteers. They yelled out that the old horse wasn't even good enough for the slaughterhouse.

Linda and the other volunteers ignored the rude comments as they studied the new rescue horse. In the glaring sunshine, they could easily count his ribs, and even the vertebrae in his spine. They weren't sure how the horse was still standing, but they were glad to help him.

Trooper moved into Linda's barn and quickly won her heart, as well as the hearts of the children who came to the barn for therapeutic riding lessons. Thanks to a diet of senior feed and beet pulp, Trooper gained weight. Within a few months, he made his debut as a therapeutic riding horse and quickly became a favorite among the young riders. Linda adopted him and today, at the age of 33, Trooper is fit and healthy. And he's still a favorite mount for therapeutic riding sessions.

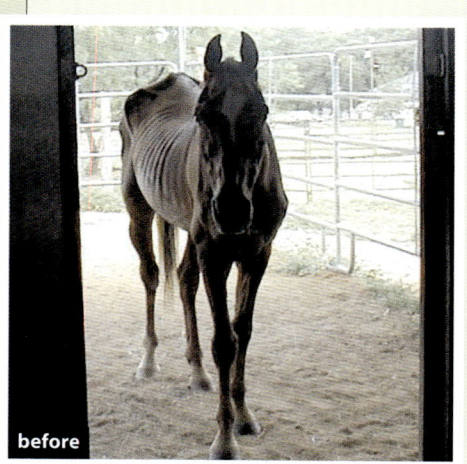

PHOTO BY LESLIE DAVIS

before

PHOTO COURTESY OF THE HELP CENTER

after

fifteen

Countdown to Rescue

Exactly how many horses can you support? Do you have an in-take procedure? There are just a few more things to consider…

You've put a lot of effort into the organization and setting up of your rescue. Everything seems to be in place, and the day you've been waiting for is finally here—you're ready to take in some needy horses (or introduce new ones to an existing herd). However, there are just a couple more things to consider: You need to determine how many horses your rescue can reasonably care for to avoid getting in over your head; and you need to make sure you have a plan for exactly how you're going to process each incoming animal.

Set Your Limits

Several factors will influence your decision on how many horses you can handle at any given time. If your rescue is based on a foster-home network, you need to consider the number of available foster homes, and the number of horses each can safely house and handle. You, or your foster-home manager, should work with each foster home to make sure it doesn't become overextended. Keep in mind that a foster-home network should always reserve a few spaces in case one of the homes can no longer foster and needs to have its horses relocated.

If your group has its own facility, you need to evaluate its capabilities. How much space do you have? Will you rely on volunteers to care for the horses, or can you afford to hire a farm manager to live on the farm and care for the horses? How many horses can the facility reasonably hold, and how many horses can the rescue's volunteers or farm manager take care of?

Regardless of whether you run a foster-home network or have your own rescue facility, you also need to determine how many horses your rescue can afford to support. Consider the cost of hay, grain, dewormers, farrier visits, and veterinary care. (*Note:* Take into consideration that malnourished horses may need extra food and supplements, and many rescued horses are likely to require additional visits from your farrier and vet.) And last but not least, don't forget to factor in the cost of facility maintenance.

Too often, horse enthusiasts jump into rescue work without first considering their limitations. Before long, they have more horses than they can handle, and the horses may be forced to go without the care they need because the rescue simply lacks the funds. In extreme cases, some rescues have become so overburdened that they could no longer provide even basic care or adequate feed. In the end, law enforcement has had go in and remove the horses yet again. So set your limits now, and stick to them so your rescue can stay afloat.

Establish an In-Take Procedure

Next, you need to develop a well-defined system, or Standard Operating Protocol (SOP), for how your group will handle each new horse, and any other equines you may opt to take in. Much of this procedure will depend on how your rescue is set up. If you'll house all the horses in your own facility, you can designate a quarantine area where the newcomers will stay until they've been examined by a veterinarian and cleared to move into one of the rescue's pastures or barns. If you'll be using a foster network, you might need to establish a quarantine facility where the horses can be housed until they've received health clearances, before moving them into foster homes. However, it's not unheard of for horses to go directly to a foster home when the rescue doesn't have a quarantine setup. (Later in the chapter, I'll provide details on what can be done to prevent the spread of disease in these cases.)

Regardless of the type of organization you run, the first part of your horse-processing SOP should address gathering basic paperwork and information. Start a file for each horse. If the horse is donated, require the owner to complete and sign a donation contract before the horse is delivered to your farm or a foster home. A donation contract may include a request that the owner supply all medical, training, and competitive history for the horse, along with a statement that transfers ownership of the horse to your rescue. For horses placed with rescue by the courts (e.g., seized horses, abandoned or stray horses), get a copy of the court order that awards custody of the horse to your rescue. In addition to this paperwork, include veterinary reports and photographs of the horse in his file.

If you have a foster network, your next priority will be to seek an appropriate foster home for the horse(s). Bluebonnet maintains an e-mail list of all foster homes. When we have a horse that needs a home, our horse coordinator posts the horse's information to the list and waits to see who can take him in. The coordinator then reviews each volunteer's qualifications and selects the appropriate place for the horse. For those with special needs, the coordinator may contact individual foster caregivers who possess the necessary background and skills. For example, she'll contact foster homes with foaling experience for a pregnant mare, and look for one with experience

15 | Countdown to Rescue

handling behavioral problems for an abused, scared horse.

Your horse-processing SOP should also address precisely how each horse is handled and assessed once he arrives at the rescue. When a new horse arrives at one of Bluebonnet's foster homes, the caregiver assigns the horse a Henneke Body Condition Score (for details, see Chapter 14, page 177), and takes photographs of the horse's left and right sides, and front and rear, to place in the horse's file. If he has any brands, scars, or other identifying marks, those are also photographed for his file.

The caregiver must also complete an Equine ID Form within two weeks of receiving the horse. This form includes a description of the horse, as well as any health, lameness, or training/behavioral problems the horse exhibits. All of this information is submitted to the horse coordinator to be reviewed and kept in the horse's file.

Another part of this horse-processing SOP are your policies for veterinary procedures. Bluebonnet's veterinary-procedure policy describes what routine veterinary work will be conducted on each horse. It includes which vaccinations will be given and the timeline in which they will be administered, the routine dental work each horse will receive, and how often Coggins tests will be performed. We also describe routine care for pregnant mares and neonatal foals in this policy.

In addition to the above, Bluebonnet explains the appropriate steps to be taken by foster homes to receive approval for veterinary work, and who in the rescue can grant approval. This policy also describes the protocol for obtaining payment for veterinary work.

Plan for Quarantine

Some diseases, such as strangles and respiratory infections, are highly contagious. They're spread through body fluids and can pass rapidly from horse to horse, quickly infecting an entire herd. A horse with a nasal discharge or swollen glands at the throatlatch may be infectious and shouldn't be put with or near healthy horses. On the other hand, a horse that's recently been exposed to a disease, or is recovering, may not show symptoms even though he's still infectious. Therefore, simply placing ill horses in quarantine may not be enough to prevent the spread of disease.

To avoid infecting your entire herd, quarantine all new arrivals regardless of their lack of symptoms. Horses need to stay in quarantine at least 14 days to avoid the spread of most diseases. If you detect any signs of disease during the quarantine period (e.g., elevated temperature, discharge from eyes or nose, swollen lymph glands, coughing, or sneezing), schedule an appointment with your veterinarian to examine the horse and develop a treatment program. Then, don't move a horse who exhibits any of these symptoms out of the quarantine area until your veterinarian has given him a clean bill of health.

The best quarantine facility will be a barn with concrete floors, because they're easy to decontaminate if you discover that any of the horses are ill. Next, separate the horses to cut down on the possibility of them passing disease to one another. Your barn should have solid walls between stalls, and the horses shouldn't be allowed to hang their heads over the stall doors.

If you bring in more horses than your quarantine facility can hold, you can temporarily use a pasture. However, don't mix horses that arrived at different times, unless you plan to keep all of them in the pasture together until the 14-day quarantine period has passed. Additionally, avoid putting any healthy horses into a pasture that's been used for quarantine for at least one month.

Since the horses will be staying in the quarantine facility for up to two weeks, it's ideal for each stall to have a door that opens into an individual turnout. To avoid nose-to-nose contact between horses in adjacent stalls/turnouts, alternate the turnout time for neighboring horses, putting each one

15 | *Countdown to Rescue*

Turnout Paddocks

A.M.	P.M.	A.M.	P.M.	
Stall	Stall	Stall	Stall	Feed Storage

Stall	Stall	Stall	Stall	Equipment Storage
A.M.	P.M.	A.M.	P.M.	

Turnout Paddocks

out for half the day (see diagram above). That way you'll always have an empty paddock between each horse during turnout time, while allowing all of them exercise time and access to sunshine.

Quarantine Stalls with Turnout Areas

While caring for horses in quarantine, be aware that you can easily carry diseases from one horse to another on your shoes, clothes, or skin, so consider limiting the number of personnel allowed to access the horses in quarantine. You may find it helpful to locate the quarantine area along the side or back of your property so people won't be tempted to pass through it on their way to other areas. (*Note:* Some rescues even set up their quarantine facility on a separate piece of property.) All the necessary feed and equipment should be kept in the quarantine barn and shouldn't be used for non-quarantined horses, and each quarantined horse should have his own bucket, water, etc.

Anything that must be taken out of the quarantine facility should first be disinfected.

All those who are working in the quarantine area should be careful to keep contaminants off their clothes. You can require those volunteers to wear coveralls that stay in quarantine, or you can require that those who take care of the quarantined horses visit them last, before going home to change clothes and shower. To further reduce the risk of spreading disease, volunteers and employees should wash off their shoes in a shoe bath and carefully wash their hands and arms before leaving the quarantine area.

The quarantine needs for a horse without a current, negative Coggins test (for Equine Infectious Anemia, or EIA), and for one who's had a positive Coggins test are different. EIA is not preventable or curable, and it can be deadly. Horses in Texas that have been diagnosed with EIA (tested positive) must be euthanized, sent to slaughter, or kept quarantined at least 200 yards from uninfected horses for the remainder of their lives. Laws for handling EIA-positive horses may vary from state to state, so check with your state veterinarian.

If a horse at your rescue tests positive for EIA, your entire facility will be quarantined for 60 days or more, and all horses on the property will have to be tested. This government-imposed quarantine means no new horses can enter the rescue's facility or foster home, and no horses can be moved out. To avoid the threat of a lengthy quarantine, many rescues refuse to take in horses without a current Coggins test, and almost none will take in a horse that's EIA-positive.

If Bluebonnet receives a horse without a Coggins, we immediately take him to a veterinarian, preferably one who can perform an in-house test. That way we have the results within an hour. However, many veterinarians need to send the blood to an outside laboratory, which can take up to a week for results. In those cases, we leave the horse with the veterinarian until we know the outcome of the test. When we seize a large group of horses, we have Coggins tests performed right away, and then house the group away from others until we receive the test results.

Don't Overlook Zoonoses

When considering quarantine procedures to prevent the spread of disease from horse to horse, you also need to consider the potential for disease to spread from horse to human. Zoonoses are diseases that can be transmitted from animals to humans. (For more information, see the chart on page 193. You might want to post this chart at the entrances to your quarantine area.)

Although it's rare for humans to contract these diseases, consider limiting volunteer contact with new horses, especially those with unknown health histories. Remind your volunteers to carefully wash their hands and any exposed skin after handling horses—especially before eating or drinking. When handling infected horses, urge your volunteers to change clothes and shower before eating and drinking or handling other animals. Do not allow human food into the quarantine barn or on any property where you're assisting law enforcement with a seizure.

Common Zoonoses

Following are the most common types of diseases that can be spread from horse to human. Included are the signs an infected horse may exhibit, and how human caretakers can protect themselves from becoming infected.

Zoonosis	Signs of Disease in Horses	Preventive Measures for Caretakers
Salmonella	Severe diarrhea, vomiting, nausea, abdominal pain, and high fever	If possible, wear gloves; always wash your hands thoroughly after handling infected horses and/or their feed/water buckets, etc.
Encephalitis	Lethargy, fever, and dementia	Use topical insecticides that protect against mosquitoes and ticks.
Rabies	Colic; lameness; slobbering (due to difficulty swallowing); neurological problems, including bizarre gait/staggering, depression, or excitability; convulsions	Anyone who handles new horses or participates in seizures should discuss a rabies vaccination with his/her doctor. Infection is spread through saliva, so extreme caution should be taken to avoid getting bitten.
Ringworm	Patchy hair loss without itching	If possible, wear gloves; change your clothing and thoroughly wash your hands (and any other exposed skin) immediately after coming into contact with affected horses.
Leptospirosis	Normally seen along with abortion or ureitis. Symptoms include mild fever and loss of appetite but can be more severe.	Change your clothing, including your shoes, and thoroughly wash your hands (and any other exposed skin) before handling other animals.
Vesicular stomatitis (VS)	Blisters/sores on the lips/gums, the udder of lactating mares, and on the tip of the penis; sometimes accompanied by swelling/blistering of the coronary bands.	Horse to human transmission is rare, but it is better to err on the side of safety. Exact transmission from animal to animal (or human) is not clearly understood. However when handling horses infected, wear gloves.
Brucellosis	Most often seen as "fistulous withers," which are swollen areas over the withers that ooze pus	If possible, wear gloves; wash your hands thoroughly after coming into contact with any body fluids.

The Road to Health

When new horses come into the rescue, you'll need to determine what kind of care each one will need. In addition to the routine veterinary care outlined in our veterinary procedures policy (for details, refer to Chapter 4, page 53), Bluebonnet also asks a veterinarian to treat any current health problems a horse may exhibit. This includes lumps, lameness, breathing problems, or old injuries. We also ask the veterinarian to check the horses for heart murmurs and to determine their overall health. (*Note:* Some rescues also have their veterinarians routinely perform blood work to check liver and kidney function, as well as look for infections in malnourished horses.)

Getting incoming horses on a consistent deworming and farrier schedule is of utmost importance. For horses that are emaciated, infested with worms, or with an unknown deworming history, we follow a schedule outlined by our veterinarian. We first deworm with a mild product, then follow up with a second dose one week later. Two weeks after the second dose, we use an ivermectin-based dewormer. After that, we deworm all horses every two months. However, because the needs of horses in different regions can vary, you'll need to work with your veterinarian to devise a program that works for your rescue.

Next, we address the horses' feet. Many horses that come into rescue have received poor hoof care, so getting their feet in shape is a priority to help avoid lameness or infection. When we receive a horse that's difficult to handle, we may delay the first farrier visit to give us time to gain his trust. However, if a horse's hooves are overly long or he's lame, we'll work with our farrier and veterinarian to tranquilize him so his feet can be trimmed as soon as possible.

Horses who haven't received regular hoof care for years may require trimming as often as every two to three weeks to gradually shorten their hooves, or may need shoes to help correct lameness problems. On the other hand, if a horse's hooves are in pretty good shape, your farrier may suggest that the horse can be maintained with a routine hoof-care schedule of every six to eight weeks.

And finally, we put together a rehabilitation program. Unless your veterinarian has extensive training in equine nutrition, or experience working with starved horses, he may not be the best source of information when you begin planning a rehabilitation program for emaciated horses. Instead, contact your local agriculture extension office to see if it can refer you to an equine nutritionist in your area.

When a starved horse arrives at your rescue, you may be tempted to start pouring grain and supplements in his feed bucket to help him gain weight quickly and regain his health. Unfortunately, such overfeeding can lead to colic, founder, and possibly even death. For this reason, healthy weight gain in horses is slow; it can take as much as six months to completely rehabilitate a severely neglected horse, especially if he's old or ill.

Dr. Carolyn Stull of the University of California at Davis has researched re-feeding starved horses. Her research compared three diets: oat hay, complete feed, and alfalfa hay. Horses fed a diet of alfalfa hay gained weight and suffered fewer health problems than those fed either complete feed or oat hay during rehabilitation. Dr. Stull recommends feeding small amounts of alfalfa hay multiple times throughout each day, gradually increasing the amount fed at each meal until the horse is eating free-choice alfalfa. In general, this process takes about two weeks. *Note:* She doesn't include any grain in her feeding program.

Depending on where you're located, you may have trouble finding quality alfalfa. If so, you can opt for a feeding program similar to that used by many of our foster homes. Although this feeding program has never been scientifically tested, we've used it to successfully rehabilitate many horses.

We start with free-choice grass hay. After two to three days, we add several small meals of grain. We start young horses with a feed specifically

15 *Countdown to Rescue*

> **DIFFERENT NEEDS FOR DIFFERENT STEEDS**
>
> **Donkeys and mules have a different metabolism than horses, making it necessary to take a different approach to their rehabilitation. Feeds that are healthy for horses can trigger severe colic and laminitis in donkeys and mules. Therefore, you should begin their rehabilitation with small amounts of grass hay several times each day. After a week, you can add in small amounts of a low-protein feed (less than 10 percent) two times each day. (*Note:* Avoid all feeds that contain molasses because it can lead to laminitis in donkeys.) You need to be patient with donkeys and mules as it can take much longer to rehabilitate them than a horse.**

formulated for their needs, such as Purina Mills Equine Junior; the others receive a complete, pelleted feed, such as Purina Mills Equine Senior. The horses are fed three to five grain meals each day. We increase each meal every third day until they are getting one to two pounds of feed at each feeding, and decrease the number of feedings (while increasing the amount per feeding). During the entire rehabilitation process we provide the horses with free-choice hay. *Note:* Donkeys and mules require a different program than horses. For more information see "Different Needs for Different Steeds," above.

We feed few additional supplements to our horses. Some people believe that adding vitamins and other grain supplements will help an emaciated horse gain weight more quickly, but we believe that a good feeding program, using quality hay and grain, will help a horse gain weight at a safe rate. That said, we do use joint supplements for horses that are arthritic, and we may use a vitamin supplement for emaciated foals or pregnant mares.

You're on Your Way

It's always an exciting event when a new horse comes into the rescue. You'll have hopes that you can make a difference in his life, and you will—if you follow an established procedure that's designed to meet individual needs. That procedure should include the following:

- Quarantine time
- A Coggins test (if there's no record of one)
- Basic veterinary workup
- Deworming program
- Trimming/shoeing program
- Feeding program.

It'll also help you track the condition of animals in your care. Use the Henneke Body Condition Scoring Chart and teach your volunteers to do so as well.

Samantha

Samantha is a pretty pony mare who now sports a bright red coat and a stunning flaxen mane and tail. When she arrived at the rescue, she was several hundred pounds underweight—her hips jutted out at sharp angles, her neck was thin, the bones of her shoulders were clearly visible, and you could count not only her ribs, but also the vertebrae in her neck and back. What's unusual is that Samantha wasn't removed from neglectful owners. In fact, no one knew who her owners were!

Law-enforcement officers responded to a call of loose horses. When they arrived, they found Samantha and a three-year-old stallion named Sam wandering down the road, stopping to eat grass on the shoulder. The deputy went from ranch to ranch, trying to locate the pair's owner, but no one claimed them. Finally after several weeks, the county sent the pair to auction, in accordance with state estray laws. The two horses were so skinny that no one wanted them, so a member of the rescue purchased them and donated them to the rescue.

Samantha gained weight, and before long her foster caretaker discovered she was broke to ride. A petite mare at only 13 hands, Samantha is calm enough under saddle to eventually make some child or small teenager a fabulous pony. And to think she was found wandering the back roads of a remote Texas county, starving and unwanted.

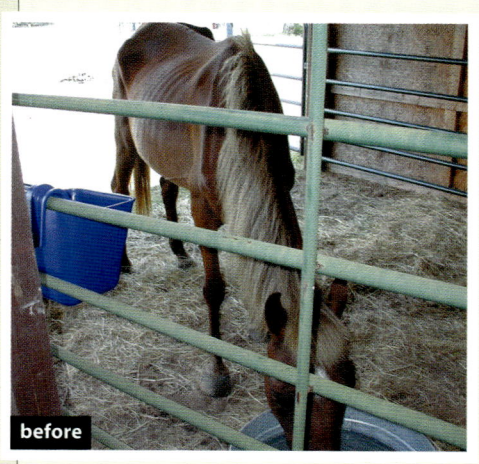

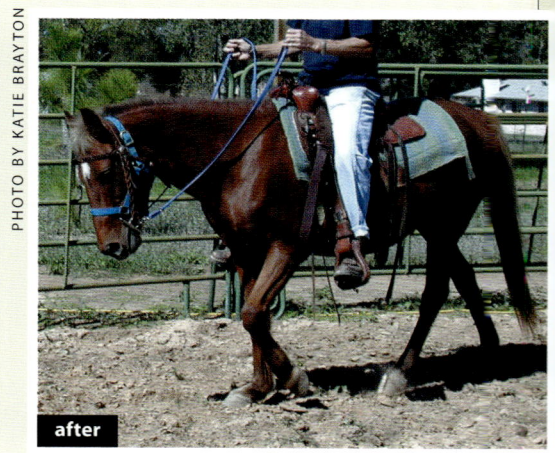

PHOTO BY DOTTIE CLOWER — before

PHOTO BY KATIE BRAYTON — after

sixteen

Disaster Preparedness

Use these ideas to help keep your volunteers, your horses, and yourself safe during a natural disaster.

Thoughts of a natural disaster strike fear into the hearts of most horse owners. We've seen the horrific scenes on the news: people leading frightened horses out of the path of raging wildfires, horses standing in chest-deep flood waters or on tiny islands of dry land, the sheer devastation of hurricanes, and the heart-wrenching pictures of animals left behind to fend for themselves. While preparation won't prevent a natural disaster, it can provide you and your animals with the best chance of escaping. Furthermore, when you have a natural-disaster plan in place, you're better equipped to help others.

Your specific disaster-preparedness plan will depend on where you're located and how your organization is set up. The first thing you need to do is recruit an Emergency Preparedness Coordinator. (See "The Role of Emergency Preparedness Coordinator," on page 200.) This is a big job with a lot of responsibility, so you'll need to find someone who's level-headed and well-organized, as well as ready and able to jump into action at a moment's notice.

16 | *Disaster Preparedness*

THE ROLE OF EMERGENCY PREPAREDNESS COORDINATOR

If your organization has a foster-home network, the EP coordinator's responsibilities will be:

- To design an evacuation plan for the horses located at foster homes, and to oversee any necessary evacuations
- To network with state agencies so your organization is ready and able to provide assistance to others
- To be accessible by phone and Internet during emergencies
- To work with your PR Coordinator (for job description, refer to Chapter 6, page 70) to distribute press releases and talk to the media
- To work with the rescue's horse coordinator or manager to maintain an up-to-date list of where each horse is located, along with pertinent information on all foster homes
- To ensure that all foster homes have an emergency-preparedness plan, including information on how to identify their horses and where to go if they need to evacuate
- To provide each foster home with information on how to put together a first-aid kit, and whom to notify in the event they must evacuate, or a horse is injured or killed during a natural disaster
- To maintain contact with the foster homes and provide support during a natural disaster
- To assist foster homes with trailering or housing for their horses

If your rescue has its own facility, the EP coordinator will work with your facility manager. In these circumstances his/her responsibilities will be:

- To design an evacuation plan for all the horses housed at the facility
- To stay informed as to the number of horses at the facility at all times, and to be aware of any horses with special needs
- To research evacuation routes from the facility
- To ensure that the facility maintains a stocked first-aid and disaster kit (see pages 205 and 206), as well as plenty of hay, grain, and water at all times
- To provide the ranch with information on how to identify each horse
- To maintain a list of all volunteers who can help load and trailer horses.

Regardless of whether your organization is composed of a foster-home network or you have your own facility, a consideration of major importance is how you're going to identify your animals. During a natural disaster fences may be blown down or knocked over by trees, and gates may be blown open, allowing your horses to roam free. If no one is at your facility or foster homes when relief workers arrive, they may need to evacuate your horses and take them to an emergency holding facility. In all of these scenarios, you'll need to have a clear-cut method to identify your horses in the event of any emergency situation. Let's take a look at the various methods you can use to accomplish this.

Hot-iron and freeze-branding. One of the easiest ways to establish the identity of your horses is to brand them when they come into your rescue. Be sure to keep copies of all brand records at the facility or foster home where each horse lives, and another copy at a separate location.

Both of these options provide permanent identification of your horses, and their visibility will enable you to identify your horses from a distance. In hot-iron branding, a heated metal brand is applied to the horse's body (generally on the hip or shoulder), burning a permanent scar into the hide.

While hot-iron branding is painful, freeze-branding appears to be less so. For this procedure, the irons are chilled using liquid nitrogen, then applied to the horse's hide. The cold irons kill the pigment, causing the hair to grow in white. For white or light-colored horses, the irons are held against the hide for a longer period of time, killing the hair follicle so there's no hair regrowth in the branded area. If you opt to brand your horses, check with your state agriculture department and county clerk to determine whether you need to register your brand.

Tattoos. While this method doesn't provide a mark that's identifiable from a distance, it's still a good way to permanently mark your horses. Tattoos, generally consisting of a series of numbers or symbols, are applied to the inside of a horse's lip. They're often used for racehorses, with the numbers generally identifying the horse's registration number and the year he was born. If you're interested in lip tattooing, talk to your veterinarian and then determine how you'll mark your horses.

Microchips. If tattoos aren't for you, consider microchips. These are tiny transponders that are implanted in a horse's neck. Each microchip has a unique code that can be read by a scanner to provide the owner's name, address, and phone number, along with other important information. Microchips are invisible and are injected with a needle, much like a vaccination, so your veterinarian may be able to do this for you. Microchips seem to be the least painful method of permanent identification.

Other ID options. Some organizations choose not to permanently identify their animals. For many it's too expensive, especially if they have several horses to brand, tattoo, or microchip at once. Others worry that the methods of permanent ID may injure or hurt their horses. Regardless of whether or not your rescue decides to permanently identify the horses, having good, clear photographs of each horse can aid in identifying them in the event of a natural disaster.

The set of photographs should include views from the front, back, left side, and right side. If a horse has any scars, brands, or other identifying marks, photograph those, too. Keep a copy of the photographs at your rescue facility or foster home, and another set in a separate location. Update photos annually because horses' coats can fade or change as they age. Also take photos during both the summer and the winter as some horses' winter coats look much different from their summer coats.

For horses without permanent IDs, there are several options for temporarily marking your horses if you're in the path of a hurricane, wildfire, or flood.

- Use a grease marker (commonly used for cattle, and available at many feed

or livestock stores) to write your phone number on your horses' sides.
- Purchase fetlock bands (available from some mail-order tack catalogs), write your phone number with a permanent marker, and put them on each horse.
- Purchase neck ID bands (available at feed stores), write your phone number on the bands with a permanent marker, and put them on each horse.
- Purchase ear tags (used for cattle), write your phone number on the tags with a permanent marker, and braid them into the horses' manes or tails.
- Put contact and medical information into a plastic baggie and braid it into the horses' manes or tails. (*Note:* Do not include a copy of Coggins tests in these baggies, as this will enable people to transport your horses out of state or sell them at auction.)
- Have halter name plates engraved with your phone number and make sure each horse is wearing a halter.

Prepare an Evacuation Plan

Identifying your horses now is just one way to prepare your rescue organization and protect your horses in the event of an emergency. You also need to determine where the rescue and its foster homes can take horses in the event of an evacuation. For groups that run a foster-home program, you may be able to evacuate horses in the affected area to foster homes in a safe area. However, in the event that your entire foster-home network needs to evacuate, or you need to evacuate your facility, compile a list of possible evacuation locations. When faced with a crisis, you'll be prepared and this list will save you time.

To plan ahead, have your EP coordinator contact other rescue organizations, county and state fairgrounds, and large boarding stables to find out if they have facilities where you could house your group's horses during a

16 | Disaster Preparedness

natural disaster. Since you never know what area will be affected, your coordinator also needs to locate facilities in various areas. She should develop a list of facilities that can house horses, and confirm each year that these facilities are still willing to assist you. In the event of a natural disaster, your EP coordinator will then be able to make arrangements for your horses to be housed, and can quickly move on to working with foster homes and volunteers to get the rescue's horses transported to the temporary facilities.

Your EP coordinator's next job is to maintain a list of volunteers who can transport horses during evacuations. If your group uses foster homes, some of them may not have a trailer, or it may be too small to transport all of their horses. Rescues with their own facilities will need volunteers to help transport all the horses out of there. The emergency-volunteer list should include how many horses each volunteer can trailer, where they're located, and emergency contact information. To create a larger list of volunteers, your coordinator can call local horse clubs and groups to recruit extra help for emergencies. She should periodically check with all volunteers on the list to see if they're still available.

Once your coordinator has a list of evacuation facilities and a list of volunteers willing to help evacuate the horses, she needs to develop a comprehensive evacuation plan. This should include:

- A complete list of evacuation facilities, including address, phone number, and directions
- A complete list of volunteers who are able to trailer horses, including their emergency contact information
- A complete list of all horses in the rescue and their location
- Maps of evacuation routes
- A copy of necessary health papers for each horse
- A means to identify each horse (e.g., information on any brand or tattoo, photographs, or materials to apply a temporary ID to each horse).

Preparedness Tips

Your EP coordinator should make sure all volunteers know the rescue's evacuation protocol. If you run a facility, post the evacuation plan in the feed room, tack room, office, and barns. Being prepared for a natural disaster can help to ensure your horses' safety, so keep these other tips in mind.

First, make sure you have enough halters and lead ropes for all the horses on the property, and make sure that each horse has a halter that fits. Every horse should know how to lead and load—but if you have feral or unhandled horses at your facility or foster home, make sure you have the ability to load them (e.g., using either fence panels or a chute) and a stock trailer to transport them. Maintain current Coggins tests and vaccinations for each horse. Evacuation facilities may not let your horses onto their property without this information. Plus, mosquito-borne diseases, such as sleeping sickness and West Nile virus, are often a problem immediately following a hurricane or flood. A current tetanus vaccination is also important because it's easy for horses to get hurt during natural disasters.

Don't let your facility run out of feed. Keep enough hay and grain on hand to feed all your horses for at least three to four days; enough for a week or more would be better. If you have horses that require supplements or medication, make sure you have enough to last two weeks. During a natural disaster, your facility or foster home may remain intact, but feed stores may be destroyed or roads blocked. Keeping enough feed on hand will ensure that your horses won't be deprived even if you can't get feed immediately after the storm has passed.

Another crucial item for

Disaster Preparedness Kit

- **Flashlights (and spare batteries)**
- **A first-aid kit for horses and humans**
- **Items used to mark/identify horses (discussed on pages 202-203)**
- **Medications and supplements**
- **Spare halter and lead rope**

disaster preparedness is a well-stocked first-aid kit for horses. (For a list of necessary items to be included, see "Emergency First-Aid Kit," below.) Keep in mind, your veterinarian may be unable to get to you during a natural disaster. If you run a foster-home network, require that all your foster homes maintain a first-aid kit and make sure you have one at your facility. This kit should travel with the horses when they're evacuated.

When There's No Time to Evacuate

While you can't be prepared for everything, having an evacuation plan, horses that are ready to trailer, and a first-aid kit can help you avoid life-threatening delays. Unfortunately, sometimes there's not enough warning to accomplish an evacuation, but if you have to stay put, there are still a few things you can do to help your animals.

First, decide whether you want to leave your horses in their stalls or leave them outside. There are advantages and disadvantages to both, and you

Emergency First-Aid Kit

- Disinfectant (e.g., alcohol or peroxide)
- Antiseptic scrub (e.g., Betadine)
- Wound powder/ointment (e.g., Cut-Heal® or Corona Ointment)
- Antibiotic aerosol (e.g., Farnam's Furall Aerosol)
- Fly repellent
- Elastikon or a similar type of porous, adhesive tape for securing bandages
- Sheet cotton
- Epsom salts
- Scissors
- Pocket knife
- Vetrap or a similar type of elasticized, self-adhesive bandage material
- Tweezers or forceps
- Thermometer
- Vaseline
- Banamine (to be used under a vet's direction)
- Butazolidan or "Bute" (to be used under a vet's direction)
- Stethoscope
- Flashlight and batteries

need to decide which is best in your situation. If you leave your horses in the barn, they'll be protected from rain, hail, falling trees, and flying objects. However, if your barn is struck by lightning, or destroyed by a tornado or hurricane-force winds, the horses may not escape. Another concern is flooding, which could trap stabled horses in their stalls.

Horses left in a pasture will be safe if your barn is destroyed, and may be able to swim out of flood water, but they may be in danger from falling trees or flying debris. Falling trees can knock over a fence, letting the horses out, or they can down power lines in your pasture, putting your horses at risk of electrocution.

Next, make sure you have plenty of drinking water. If your area is hit, you may lose water services. Fill any water buckets and troughs you have, even if you don't normally use them. You can store water in trash cans, buckets, and bathtubs. Storing water can help hold you over until water services are restored.

Another invaluable item is a generator, but make sure you always have adequate fuel on hand to operate it. Also keep flashlights or battery-powered lanterns and extra batteries in a place where they're easily accessible. You should also keep an ax, crowbar, and chainsaw (with fuel) handy. These items may enable you to remove trees or debris from your driveway or fence line, and they may help you save a horse caught beneath debris.

Do Unto Others....

Now that you've done your best to prepare for natural disasters, you might also consider what you can do to help others. If you're not in the path of a natural disaster, you may be able to open up your facility to horses that need to be evacuated. Make sure each horse's owner leaves his contact information and permission to call a veterinarian in the event his horse needs it. Or maybe you'd be able to volunteer to trailer horses. You can join the Humane Society of the U.S. (HSUS), the American Society for the Prevention of Cruelty to Animals (ASPCA), or other local groups to volunteer your services. Check in with your state livestock and veterinary associations to see if they maintain a list of volunteers that are willing to help house and transport horses in the event of a natural disaster. If you can't find a list of volunteers, you may want to contact other horse groups across your state and work to establish a database of individuals who're willing to help.

Your organization could also be called upon to assist horse owners after a natural disaster has passed. You might work with law enforcement and rescue workers to retrieve horses that were left behind when their owners evacuated, or horses that got loose during the storm. You might need to house these horses or volunteer to help out at a holding facility. Volunteers may be needed to take hay, grain, and other supplies to horse owners. Again, check with your state livestock association, county extension agents, and state veterinary association to see what kind of assistance you can offer.

Regardless of the size of your rescue, being prepared for natural disasters can save the lives of your horses. Use these ideas to help keep yourself, your volunteers, and your horses safe during a natural disaster.

Dream Girl

The sign hanging at the tack store read: "Free foal—due next month. Call (XXX) XXX-XXXX." Our volunteer wondered why anyone would be searching for a home for an unborn foal, so she called the number as she left the tack store. She learned that the mare had become pregnant while at a trainer's property and the owner didn't want the foal. In fact, she told the mare's new trainer to euthanize the foal when it was born so the mare could get back to work. The trainer hated the thought of killing an innocent baby, so she hung the sign in the tack store and hoped the foal could find a home.

Our volunteer called me and asked if we could take the foal. We weren't quite ready to start taking in horses yet, but how could I say no? The baby deserved a chance at a good life, and I felt we could give her that chance.

Our volunteer then spoke to the mare's owner, who said she wanted us to come get the foal as soon as it was born. She wasn't willing to let the foal nurse or spend any time with its dam. (She later relented and agreed to let the foal nurse long enough to receive the antibody-rich colostrum, or first milk, but she wouldn't let her stay more than a few days.)

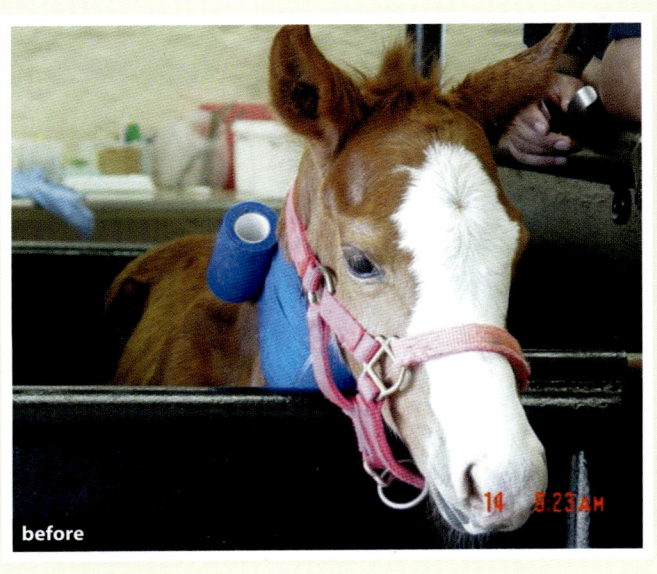

before

The day the mare foaled, the trainer called our volunteer to let her know. She rushed over to meet the baby, a filly she named Dream Girl. A few days later, she returned along with her horse trailer to take Dream Girl home. Since Dream Girl was far too young to be weaned from her dam, our volunteer had bottles and milk replacer ready for her.

Unfortunately, Dream Girl didn't like drinking from a bottle or a bucket, and she didn't like the milk replacer, either. Her foster family tried introducing her to a "wet mare" (one that's lactating), but the two didn't get along and Dream Girl couldn't nurse. Despite her foster "dad's" coaxing, Dream Girl wouldn't drink and grew weak.

Dream Girl ended up receiving IV fluids at the veterinarian's office several times. Her foster dad began spending several hours every day squirting milk replacer into her mouth with a syringe. After several months of touch-and-go health, Dream Girl finally began eating and drinking on her own.

By this time, the little filly's foster family had spent so many hours with her and had worried about her so much, that they couldn't stand the thought of her leaving their farm. They adopted her, and now they're enjoying showing off their beautiful rescue filly—the one that was almost euthanized at birth by a cruel, careless owner.

PHOTO BY WENDY TAYLOR

after

seventeen

Develop an Adoption Program

A well-planned adoption process will help you identify the best homes for your horses.

Unless you run a sanctuary or retirement facility, where horses and other equines come to live out their lives, your organization—and your horses—will benefit from a well-planned adoption program. You'll need to determine how you'll evaluate horses, what your adoption fees will be, and what you'll require from potential adopters. Let's take a careful look at these issues, and other considerations, before you put your first horse up for adoption.

The Evaluation Process

1. Evaluate temperament. Before you can put a horse up for adoption, you need to determine what type of adopter will be best for him. At Bluebonnet, our foster caretakers observe new horses to help us determine each one's temperament. They may spend several weeks watching a new horse and interacting with him, then report their observations to the rescue. This information is added to each horse's Web page, and given to any potential adopters. Fosters carefully watch the following behaviors:

How the horse interacts with other horses. Is the horse submissive—does he run away from every horse he meets? Or is he the dominant horse in the pasture—kicking and biting other horses to get his way? If he's dominant, is he the passive or aggressive type? Passively dominant horses will pin their ears and threaten to kick or bite. In response to this behavior other horses move out of their way. Aggressively dominant horses will chase other horses, corner them, and kick or bite them.

A horse's interaction with other horses will help you determine the type of person that would be best-suited to adopt him. For example, an aggressive horse may not be a good fit for a novice horseperson, may need to be housed with horses that will stick up for themselves, or may even need to be kept separated from other horses.

How the horse interacts with people. Is he a shy horse that avoids humans? Does he run away when you attempt to catch him, and/or flinch when you touch him? Or, does he come running up to people, looking for a pet and some treats? Does he treat humans like other horses—jostling them, pinning his ears at them, and threatening to bite and kick when a person asks him to do something—or does he respect humans?

A shy horse may need a quiet, patient adopter who can spend time building his confidence. A horse that treats humans like other horses needs an experienced adopter who can teach him to respect a human's space.

The horse's trainability. When you try to teach him something new, does he learn quickly, or do you need to repeat each lesson several times? When you begin a new day of training, has he forgotten what he learned before, or is he able to move on to the next lesson? You can judge a horse's trainability when you're simply handling him and teaching him to lead or tie; you don't have to attempt to teach him groundwork or begin training him to ride to evaluate trainability.

A horse's ability and/or willingness to learn will also indicate the type of adopter he'll need. A slow horse requires someone with patience who doesn't mind repeating lessons, while the horse that's a quick learner would be a better candidate for the person who wants to get a horse trained quickly so she can begin competing or riding.

How the horse reacts to new things. Does he look at a new object and continue on, or does he spook, spin around, and bolt? A spooky horse is going to need a confident, experienced rider, while a laid-back horse that takes everything in stride would be more appropriate for a novice or timid rider.

2. Evaluate riding or driving capabilities. If a horse is lame or has health problems, you'll need to discuss his limitations with your veterinarian. For example, horses with COPD (chronic obstructive pulmonary disease, or heaves), asthma, or anhydrosis (inability to sweat) may be limited in their use, depending on the severity of the disease and type of weather in which they would be working. (Very hot and/or humid weather is typically bad for horses with any of these diseases.) These horses may need to stop working during the summer, or may be restricted to riding at a walk and short trot for only a few minutes a day. The type of medication they require can also influence how much work they can tolerate.

Many lameness issues can be corrected with proper trimming/shoeing and rest, but you'll need to discuss specific cases with your veterinarian to get his opinion on treatment and prognosis. In the past, veterinarians and horse owners believed that both founder and navicular disease ended a horse's "useful" career, and they often euthanized horses with either condition. However, we can now manage these conditions, as well as arthritis, with correct shoeing or trimming, medications, and proper exercise. While a horse that's obviously and consistently lame may not be suitable for a riding horse, those that exhibit only occasional lameness may be fine for infrequent, short

17 | Develop an Adoption Program

rides. Your veterinarian can help you determine the amount of work, if any, each horse can handle.

You'll also need to take a horse's age into consideration when determining his abilities. While many people retire older horses, not all horses are happy to retire. "Yellow" was such a horse. He served his owners as a ranch horse for years—and had scars from being gored by a bull to prove it. When Yellow turned 25, his owners stopped using him for ranch work and turned him out to pasture.

Yellow began to slowly lose weight even though he had access to plenty of grass and good food. His owners decided to humanely euthanize him because they didn't want him to slowly starve to death. They took him to their veterinarian to be put down, but when the veterinarian learned that Yellow was sound, and his only health problem was weight loss, she suggested that his owners give him to a rescue. When he arrived, he was underweight and depressed. But his foster home had young children who groomed him, fed him, and took him on walks. The old horse slowly gained weight, and when he was healthy enough to be ridden they starting taking him on short rides. Yellow really blossomed—he filled out and his coat shone.

Yellow lost weight and energy when he was retired because he was depressed. Although his age limited his ability to take the hard riding that ranch work required, he was happy with light riding by a group of children. Other horses like Yellow may need to slow down due to age, but still enjoy getting out and being ridden. Some older horses can continue competing in shows and play days, even roping, into their late 20s and even 30s. Each horse's individual needs should be taken into consideration. If a horse has age-related problems, such as arthritis in his back, he may need to retire, but horses shouldn't automatically be "put out to pasture" when they reach a certain age. Many older horses make great riding horses until the end of their lives.

On the other end of the age spectrum, you may also need to limit the amount of riding young horses can handle. Bluebonnet prefers that horses aren't started under saddle until they're three to four years old. Our veterinarians have also instructed us to give severely malnourished foals even longer to grow up and mature—advising us to wait until they're four to five years old before carrying a rider.

3. Evaluate level of training. For this, we ask an experienced person from one of our foster homes, or a trainer, to ride and observe the horse. If he appears to be broke to ride and doesn't appear to have any training problems, we ask the evaluator to ride the horse in a variety of situations, such as in a round pen and an arena, in an open field, around other horses, and on trails, if possible. The more we know about a horse's training level, the better equipped we'll be to select a good adoptive placement. We avoid placing green or untrained horses with novice horse owners and beginning riders, unless they'll be working with a qualified trainer/instructor.

4. Evaluate health and soundness. This means working with our veterinarian and farrier to correct or treat any health or lameness problems. We also keep good records of any conditions that were treated, including what was done and when so we can provide this information to potential adopters. In addition to this, we make sure all of our horses receive the following before being put up for adoption:
- Coggins test
- Vaccinations—we administer flu/rhino, rabies, VEWT (Venezuelan/Eastern/Western Encephalitis and Tetanus), and West Nile Virus. However, horses in different regions may require different vaccinations.
- Regular farrier care
- Regular deworming
- Dental work (e.g., teeth floating), as necessary.

17 | Develop an Adoption Program

The Adoption Process

1. Determine a fee. Rescues have various ways to set adoption fees, and different reasons for setting them. Although there are a few organizations that don't charge an adoption fee, most rescues use the money from adoptions to help offset some of the expenses of rescuing and rehabilitating the horse, as well as to help others in need. One rescue reports that they used to adopt out horses without an adoption fee, but came to believe that these horses had no perceived value to their new owners, and that they often rushed into an adoption simply because the horse was free. Often, the rescue ended up removing these horses from their adoptive homes because they weren't receiving proper care. After they instated adoption fees, they had fewer problems with adopters.

There are different ways to arrive at adoption fees. For instance, some rescues use flat fees, charging the same amount for all their horses, regardless of age, training, etc. Other organizations set fees on a case-by-case basis, trying to calculate and recuperate the amount of money they've put into each horse.

Bluebonnet, on the other hand, sets its fees based on each horse's abilities and needs. Although this means that the adoption fees for some horses won't cover their expenses, there are also horses that are adopted out for more than their expenses. We're happy when our cumulative adoption fees equal our total veterinary expenses for a year.

We do, however, have some standard adoption fees for certain types of horses: registered green-broke horses, unregistered green-broke horses, registered weanlings and yearlings, kids' horses, ponies, and more. If a horse doesn't fall into one of the standard categories, our officers research how much similar horses sell for in Texas and set an adoption fee slightly below that amount. We believe that due to the demands we place on our adopters (e.g., they can't breed the horse; they must return him if they can no longer keep him) we have to be somewhat generous with our fees, and set them lower than prices for similar horses.

2. Develop an adoption application and screening program. Almost every rescue has a slightly different adoption program, and you'll need to determine what type of program works best for your organization. Some rescues sell their horses outright—they do very little, if any, prescreening and don't retain ownership. Other organizations conduct background and credit checks on all adopters, require submission of a long adoption application, conduct annual checkups on the horse for the remainder of his life, and never relinquish ownership to the adopter.

Organizations with tough adoption procedures feel confident that they approve only the best horsemen and women. However, those organizations often miss out on wonderful adopters who simply don't wish to fill out a long application or submit to annual inspections. It seems that there's a fine line between implementing a procedure to screen out inappropriate adopters and one that doesn't drive away wonderful people. Bluebonnet has developed an adoption policy with this in mind. Our adoption procedure requires the following:

An adoption application. Information as to where the horse will be kept, the adopter's previous horse experience, how the adopter will care for the horse, and other questions that help us assess whether the adopter is a good candidate for the horse(s) he is interested in adopting.

References. Potential adoptees are required to furnish three references. One of our volunteers then calls to verify these references and talks to each one about the person who is applying to adopt.

The first and most important reference is a veterinarian. For most adopters this is the vet who currently treats their horses. If they don't own any horses, it would be the veterinarian they plan on using for their adopted horse.

17 | *Develop an Adoption Program*

This information tells us that the adopter is preparing for horse ownership and will have a veterinarian available, should one be needed.

The second reference is an equine professional, such as a farrier, trainer, riding instructor, or boarding-facility manager. We ask them to tell us how the applicant treats his horses and ask whether they would recommend the applicant as an adopter.

The third reference should come from a friend of the applicant. They're asked to describe how the applicant cares for his animals and whether they would have any reservations about letting the applicant adopt a horse.

Pre-adoption inspection. One of our volunteers visits the potential adopter and the property where he plans to keep any adopted horses. The volunteer records information about the property and notes any concerns on an inspection form. The vice president/equine coordinator reviews the form to determine whether the property is safe for horses. In some instances, the VP/EC may request that some changes be made by a potential adopter, such as cleaning up trash in the pasture, or periodically cleaning water troughs, before being approved to adopt.

Adoption contract. Once the adopter is approved and decides which horse(s) he wishes to adopt, an adoption contract is signed. The contract gives the rescue the right to inspect the horse and remove him if he's being neglected. The adopter also agrees not to breed the horse, and to return him to Bluebonnet if he/she can't keep him.

Post-adoption follow-up. Bluebonnet volunteers conduct three to four post-adoption follow-up visits at two, six, 12, and 24 months after the adoption. During these visits, the volunteer records information about the horse and the property where he lives, and takes photographs of him. The vice president/equine coordinator then reviews the notes and photographs to determine whether the horse is in good health and being properly cared for.

At first, some people think our adoption process is too difficult. But after we explain that our first and foremost concern is the long-term welfare of the horse, potential adopters usually understand. We emphasize that the procedure is low-stress, and we welcome questions at any point in the process. If we have concerns about a potential adopter, we discuss those concerns with the adopter and give him a chance to make improvements.

Many of our adopters tell us they appreciate this process, adding that it makes them feel confident that we're serious about getting good homes for our horses. Others appreciate that we insist on our horses being returned to us because they know if they can't keep their horse, we'll find another, excellent home for him.

When the Answer is "No"

Part of the screening process is denying adopters who don't meet your requirements. No one looks forward to telling an applicant they don't meet the requirements to adopt a horse, but don't put it off. Notify them by letter or e-mail in a timely manner. Let them know why you feel they don't meet your requirements and give them a chance to make changes, if possible. Some rejected adopters are happy to make improvements—sometimes the problem was something they'd simply overlooked.

If you put a lot of thought and time into developing your adoption process, it'll pay off when you begin to adopt out horses. A well-planned process will not only screen out those who cannot or will not care for your horses, but will also enable you to find wonderful, loving homes for the horses in your rescue. The joy expressed by happy adopters, along with the horses' security and well-being, makes the effort worthwhile.

eighteen

Dog and Cat Rescue

Consider the species-specific differences between small- and large-animal rescue.

In general, more people are aware of the need for dog and cat rescue than they are of the need for horse rescue. Most of us have visited a shelter or pound at some point in our lives, or know someone who has, and many of us have adopted dogs or cats from shelters. So let's take a look at the differences between rescuing small and large animals.

The Advantages of Dog and Cat Rescue

Several national organizations, such as the Humane Society of the United States (HSUS) and the American Society for the Prevention of Cruelty to Animals (ASPCA), strive to educate the public about dog and cat overpopulation and promote the adoption of stray/unwanted pets. Therefore, small-animal rescuers have an advantage over horse rescuers because there's no national group promoting awareness of neglected/unwanted horses. As a result, the first job for those who set out to rescue horses is often to educate the public about horse rescue and the benefits of adoption. Other advantages to dog and cat rescue are:

- Qualified foster caretakers and adopters are easier to find than those for horses.
- Dogs and cats require less space and their care is less expensive than that which is necessary for horses.
- Dog-training classes are readily available in most locations and they're less expensive than riding lessons and horse training.
- Small-animal veterinarians and behaviorists are also available in many areas to help owners with health problems, and behavior and training questions.
- More people own dogs and cats than horses, so rescuers have a larger pool of experienced owners from which to seek foster homes and adopters.
- More grants are available for dog and cat rescue than for horse rescue. Dog and cat organizations qualify for spay/neuter grants, in addition to grants to establish new programs or to fund existing ones. (*Note:* When horse rescuers apply for grants, they often must work hard to educate the foundation about what they do before being considered.)
- Small animal rescues may also find more businesses willing to provide corporate sponsorships—often because they better understand the needs of dog and cat rescue. As mentioned earlier, this is due to national animal-welfare groups like HSUS, which promote awareness of dog and cat overpopulation, and because more people own dogs/cats than horses.

The Disadvantages to Dog and Cat Rescue

There are many more needy dogs and cats than there are horses. The Humane Society estimates that three to four million dogs and cats are euthanized every year in shelters across the country. Other disadvantages to rescuing dogs and cats are:

- Dogs and cats are more often the victims of hoarders—people who collect several hundred animals at a time and house them in deplorable conditions.
- Dogs and cats are always at risk for extreme overbreeding. Instead of producing just one offspring a year as horses do, dogs and cats can produce up to 10 or more babies per litter, and can have more than one litter per year.
- Dogs and cats can start producing babies before they're even one year old, whereas most horses are three or four years old before they start producing foals, although fillies as young as two years of age can give birth.

Specific Considerations

If you're thinking about starting a dog or cat rescue, most of this book should be useful to you. You'll have many of the same needs as a horse rescue: You'll need to operate like a business—striving to keep your organization's finances in the black and to avoid debt; you'll need to promote your rescue; find and keep volunteers; and conduct money-making fund-raisers. However, you do have some additional considerations.

Will you run a breed-specific rescue, or one with an open-door policy?
You'll need to decide whether you want to run a breed-specific rescue or help any and all dogs or cats in need. If you wish to help a specific breed, you should contact the breed association or registry to see if they're working with a rescue group, or would be interested in doing so. Some breed associations set up their own rescue groups while others network with certain breed-specific rescues. Many breed associations provide links on their Web sites to

rescue groups, or refer people who are looking to place or adopt a dog to the rescues with which they network. If the breed association already works with a rescue, you might consider joining forces with them instead of forming your own organization, or you could offer to network with the existing group so more animals can be helped.

Next you'll need to decide whether your group will accept part-bred animals. Many dog and cat rescuers decide to limit themselves to a specific breed because they know and understand the unique needs of that breed. By restricting your group to a specific breed, and accepting only purebred animals, you'll also limit the number of animals that'll need your help. When faced with a needy dog or cat who isn't a purebred, you may find it hard to say no. However, if you establish your rescue's policies in the beginning—and stick to them—you can avoid being overrun with animals.

Will it be a "no-kill," "low-kill," or "kill" rescue? The fundamental differences between these types of rescues are:

- A *no-kill* organization is one that won't put any animals to sleep, even those that are sick or injured.
- A *low-kill* rescue will euthanize animals that are sick or injured, but some euthanize *all* ill or injured animals, while others do so only after trying to treat the animals. If a veterinarian determines the animal cannot be helped, he's then euthanized.
- A *low-kill* organization may euthanize aggressive animals they believe are too dangerous to place in adoptive homes, or may opt to house them in qualified foster homes or a sanctuary.
- A *kill* rescue will euthanize animals due to lack of space. Some kill shelters give each animal a set number of days and then euthanize him if he hasn't found a home. Others keep all animals a minimum number of days and then euthanize animals only when they need space. In this setting, some animals

are euthanized immediately after their minimum time is up because the shelter is overfull, while others stay in the rescue facility days or even weeks longer because the shelter has space available.

If you choose to run a low-kill program, you'll need to decide what criteria you'll use to help you decide whether or not to euthanize an animal. Some rescues only euthanize animals that are obviously suffering from untreatable injuries or illnesses; others set financial limits that detail the maximum amount that can be spent to treat each animal. Yet other rescues will spend whatever it takes to help an animal, and will only euthanize as a last resort.

How will you handle aggressive animals? Unfortunately, aggressive dogs can be very hard to place and they present liability concerns. If a dog that has displayed aggression in the past bites someone, your rescue can be sued. Also, you may have a very hard time finding suitable foster homes and adopters for aggressive animals. So, if you decide to place an aggressive dog, be completely honest with the adopter, fully explaining any history of aggression. If possible, include a description of what happened and the circumstances that may have prompted the aggressive behavior. For example, if you have a dog that bit someone who touched him while he was eating, explain when the behavior occurred and caution the foster owner or adopter to leave the dog alone at mealtime. (*Note:* In most cases, dogs that have bitten children shouldn't be placed in homes with children, and dogs that have attacked other dogs or cats shouldn't be placed in homes with other animals.)

If you decide that your rescue group will euthanize aggressive dogs, there are many temperament tests available, although they're a controversial topic. Supporters of temperament testing propose that it helps shelter and rescue workers determine which dogs are too aggressive to safely place in adoptive homes. They also say it provides clues as to the best type of home for the dog—with children, with other dogs, as a working dog, as an only

> **Expert's Tip**
>
> **Temperament Testing**
> When performing a temperament test, testers analyze the following:
> - **behavior during petting**
> - **behavior during interactions with humans**
> - **behavior during social interactions with other dogs**
> - **prey response/drive**
> - **play behavior**
> - **personality traits, such as calmness, playfulness, independence.**
>
> **The tester will also evaluate prior training and current trainability, which is why temperament testing is best done by someone with experience, who understands training cues and commands.**

companion, etc. (For more information, see "Temperament Testing," above.)

On the other hand, critics of temperament testing claim it doesn't take into account extraneous factors, such as how long the dog has been in the shelter, his health, or his age. They also claim that many dogs that are labeled aggressive can be retrained and safely re-homed. You should consider both sides of the temperament-testing issue before reaching a decision.

If you opt to use temperament tests, select someone who has experience in temperament testing and understands canine behavior. Before testing, wait until the dog has become acclimated to the shelter or foster home. Some dogs take longer to settle in than others, and it isn't fair to conduct temperament testing while a dog is still stressed from being re-homed.

Keep in mind that some traits, such as severe aggression, may be very difficult or impossible to correct. Dogs that repeatedly bite people, especially when the attack appears unprovoked, may be too difficult (and too risky) to retrain. Feral or wild dogs that haven't been handled and don't trust humans may continue to bite or attack, despite training and patient handling.

Fortunately, good training and handling can correct many other behavioral problems. For example, if you have a dog with a high prey drive, you don't need to euthanize him. Instead, place him in a home without children or small pets (cats, rabbits, etc.), who could stimulate those instincts with their quick movements. Dogs that are aggressive to other dogs but not to humans can be placed in homes without other dogs—as long as the adopter understands the animal's history and needs (e.g., no dog parks!).

How many animals will the law allow? Dog and cat rescuers also need to research zoning laws before opening a facility. Towns and cities often limit the number of animals that can be housed at one location. Several rescuers have been fined, and some have had their animals confiscated because they exceeded their town's animal limits. If you run a foster-home program, make sure your foster homes don't take in more animals than their city allows. Additionally, be sure to check whether or not your city or county requires a permit to run an animal rescue or a home-based business. (Even if *you* don't see your rescue as a business, your city may.) You should be able to get this information from your city hall or county courthouse.

Is your current insurance adequate? Although Chapter 12 (page 157) discussed insurance and ways to protect yourself, dog and cat rescues may have greater liability concerns than horse rescues. Dogs and cats are often more prone to bite or scratch when they're in stressful situations, such as at adoption events, when they're handled by children or strangers, and when they're introduced to new animals. Additionally, dogs and cats that live in foster homes may be exposed to new people frequently. Family members and friends visiting the foster home have close interaction with the dogs or cats living in the house, while visitors to an equine foster home may only see the horse in a stall or across the fence. If someone is hurt by one of your animals, he may sue your rescue and without adequate liability insurance your organization could be bankrupted easily.

Will you vaccinate for rabies? While it's possible for horses to contract rabies, dogs and cats are far more likely to come in contact with a rabid animal. Even if your cats are inside-only and your dogs are rarely outside, rabies should be a concern. And don't forget, you could unknowingly bring a rabid animal into your shelter and expose all of your animals. In many areas of the country, a dog or cat that bites someone, and doesn't have proof of rabies vaccinations, must be destroyed. Furthermore, most regions require that all dogs and cats be vaccinated against rabies. While vaccinations may seem like a somewhat unnecessary expense, they are an absolute necessity.

Have you considered quarantine? Quarantine and sanitation needs may be different for those running a dog or cat rescue. Feline diseases, such as feline immunodeficiency virus (FIV) and feline leukemia, are spread by body fluids. You can prevent the spread of these diseases by quarantining new arrivals until they've been tested for these diseases.

Parvovirus in dogs is also easily spread, but can be contained by quarantining new arrivals. Use kennels or cages that are kept in separate rooms, or even a separate building, for quarantine purposes—and thoroughly clean the area on a regular basis. Designate food/water bowls and kennel/cage-cleaning equipment for use only in the quarantine area. After leaving the area, be sure to carefully wash your hands, and change your clothing (or consider wearing coveralls that can be removed and left in the quarantine area). With a little work, you can keep infectious diseases from spreading.

Did you know you're more likely to catch a zoonotic disease from a dog or cat than a horse? Zoonotic diseases, or those that can be spread from animals to humans, were discussed in Chapter 15 (page 185).

The following diseases may be caught from either dogs or cats:

Zoonosis	Signs of Disease in Animals	Preventive Measures for Caretakers
Salmonella	Both humans and animals may have diarrhea, vomiting, nausea, abdominal pain, and high temperature. Humans may also have headaches and eye pain in addition to abdominal distress.	Dirty environments increase the risk of infection, so washing your hands often will help prevent it.
Rabies	Rabies causes neurological problems and eventually death.	Rabies is spread through bodily fluids—especially via saliva. If your volunteers will be handling new dogs or cats, helping catch loose dogs or cats, or assisting law enforcement in forcibly removing animals, encourage them to be vaccinated for rabies.
Ringworm	Ringworm is a skin and scalp condition that produces a ring-shaped, reddish rash that may be itchy.	Ringworm is spread through contact with affected animals. Volunteers can wear gloves when handling animals with skin conditions that resemble ringworm and should wash exposed skin after handling any animals that may have ringworm.

The following diseases may be caught from cats:

Zoonosis	Signs of Disease in Animals	Preventive Measures for Caretakers
Toxoplasmosis	Toxoplasmosis can cause fever, depression and loss of appetite in cats. Cats can also carry and spread toxoplasmosis while being asymptomatic. For humans, pregnant women who contract toxoplasmosis run a risk of aborting or giving birth to babies with congenital defects.	Cats pass toxoplasmosis to humans through their feces, so pregnant women should avoid cleaning litter boxes and kennels.
Psittacosis	In animals, signs are non-specific and include coughing, sneezing, conjunctivitis. In humans, psittacosis can lead to pneumonia.	This disease is most common in caged birds, but in cats it causes eye and respiratory infections. Transmission from cats to humans is rare. It can be transmitted via bodily fluids and placentas, so wear gloves and wash hands and exposed skin carefully after handling ill cats.
Pasteurella	One of the most common zoonotic diseases, pasteurella is passed from cats to humans via cat bites.	If you're bitten by a cat, carefully clean the wound with an antiseptic wash and apply an antibiotic ointment.
Cat Scratch Fever or Disease	Cat scratch fever produces systemic illness and lymph-node lesions.	This disease is transmitted through cat scratches and is caused by the bacteria *Rochalimaea henselae*. Avoid playing hard with cats (where they may be tempted to bite or scratch) and thoroughly wash all bites and scratches.

The following diseases may be caught from dogs:

Zoonosis	Signs of Disease in Animals	Preventive Measures for Caretakers
Sarcoptic mange or scabies	In humans this disease is often seen as a pinpoint rash on the chest and abdomen. In dogs, scabies causes itching, scabs, and hair loss.	Generally when a human gets sarcoptic mange from a dog, it causes only brief itching and does not last. Have your veterinarian treat dogs with mange and limit volunteer contact with those dogs until they've completed the treatment.
Leptospirosis	This disease causes flu-like symptoms in humans. In severe cases, it can cause infections in the kidney, liver, brain, and heart.	Leptospirosis is spread through urine-contaminated soil or water, so volunteers should wear gloves and wash exposed skin after cleaning kennels or dog runs used by dogs who have this disease.

Many zoonotic diseases are spread from contact with body fluids or contact with infected skin or sores. Washing your hands, not eating or drinking around animals, and other general sanitary practices can help reduce your risk of contracting a zoonotic disease. When cleaning litter boxes or dog kennels, wear gloves and a mask that covers your nose. Don't handle cats or dogs that haven't yet been vaccinated against rabies, wash all bites and scrapes with an antiseptic cleanser, then coat with antibiotic ointment. If you'll be handling dogs and cats that don't have rabies vaccinations, or whose histories are unknown, talk to your doctor about being vaccinated for rabies.

While many issues are similar across rescues, there are a few issues that are unique to dog and cat rescue, as we have discussed in this chapter. However, if you go into rescue work with firm plans and policies in place, and are prepared to deal with species-specific issues, you'll have the greatest chance of running a professional, successful organization.

nineteen

Wildlife and Exotic-Animal Rescue

If "vive la difference" is your motto, this type of rescue might be for you—but make sure you do your homework.

First, let's clarify the difference between "wildlife" and "exotic animals." The term "wildlife" refers to indigenous (or native) animals that are undomesticated and living in their natural habitat. Exotic animals aren't native to this country; they're imported from other areas (often overseas) and can't live in the wild here. While many areas prohibit people from keeping wildlife as pets, exotic animals are becoming popular with those who seek unusual pets as status symbols.

Although wildlife and exotic-animal rescuers share some similar problems, the differences are nonetheless quite challenging. First, the public may not understand the needs of the species these rescues help—or why they choose to help them. These animals aren't domesticated, can be dangerous to handle, and are expensive to house and feed. Secondly, federal, state, and local governments often impose restrictions on the species that wildlife and exotic rescues must house, and these rescues may be subject to licensing fees and facility inspections. But there are far bigger issues for you to consider if you want to open your doors to wildlife or exotic animals—and each type of rescue faces challenges unique to its animals.

Wildlife Rescue

Wildlife rescuers rehabilitate injured or ill wildlife, and on occasion they work with law enforcement to remove wild animals that are being kept as pets. In addition to this, every spring brings large numbers of young, orphaned animals into wildlife rescues. Their parents may have been killed, their homes may have been flooded with spring rains, or the land in their habitat may have been cleared, driving them out of the trees. Whatever the case, these orphaned babies are often so young that they require round-the-clock care and feeding, and can't survive without it.

So if you're considering running a wildlife rescue, you'll need to be prepared for orphaned animals. This includes learning about the nutritional needs (e.g., what they eat, and how often) of the species you'll be working with, and locating a source for milk replacer or formula, which can be hard to find—and expensive. (Be sure to keep plenty available in spring months.) If you'll be working with birds or reptiles, you may need worms, small mice, or other types of food. Also, some young animals will need heat lamps or heating pads to provide them with enough warmth. Raising orphans is hard work and can be emotionally and physically exhausting for volunteers.

Next, you'll have to decide whether you're going to provide sanctuary to the animals that are brought to you, or release them back into the wild once they're rehabilitated (a choice that's not an option for exotic animals). Obviously, animals that can't recover from injuries that impair their ability to hunt can't be released, but others can be—once they're strong enough to survive on their own. Consult your state's conservation department or game warden regarding the regulations concerning relocating and releasing animals, and where it would be appropriate for you to do so. It's very important to remember that human contact should be limited with animals that will be released. If they become habituated to humans and lose their natural fear, they'll be easy prey for hunters and others who may wish to harm them.

Exotic Rescue

The need for exotic-animal rescue has increased in the last few years. Some pet stores now sell exotic animals, and Internet suppliers make it easy to purchase an exotic pet. While flying squirrels and sugar gliders may be fairly easy and inexpensive to keep, foxes, large cats (e.g., lynxes and tigers), exotic deer, and others are more expensive to house and feed. Exotic pet owners often have a desire to show off a knowledge about something "different"—something their friends and family know nothing about. Unfortunately, exotic-pet owners often fail to learn about these animals before they purchase one.

What frequently happens in these cases is that when they get their new pet home, they don't provide adequate or appropriate feed, and the animal starves to death. Or, they provide inadequate housing and the animal escapes, sometimes hurting or killing other animals or people in the area. These people fail to realize that when full-grown, this exotic animal will be stronger than they are, and will not be easy to control. As a result, when this "wild" animal grows up, he sometimes kills the owner or a family member.

Exotic animals are not only readily available, but also relatively inexpensive. While shopping at a pet store a few years ago, I spotted a gorgeous large cat roaming around the store. When I got closer, I realized that this was no domestic cat—it was a lynx. The store also had a wallaby for sale and a tiger cub. I got to sit on the floor while the tiger cub climbed into my lap, and I admit that I was enthralled by him—he was adorable and tiny. He snuggled in my lap, and I was almost ready for a tiger cub of my own. Out of curiosity, I asked the store owner how much it would cost to buy one. I was amazed to find out that I could buy a tiger cub for less than what I paid for my horses. Luckily, I knew that I couldn't care for a full-grown tiger. While his purchase price might have been affordable, I couldn't afford to feed or house him. I didn't have the knowledge or facilities to take care of a tiger without endangering my own life, and I knew it wouldn't be fair to keep a wild animal—whose behavior is ruled by instincts—in a small enclosure isolated from his own species and natural habitat. Unfortunately, many other prospective exotic-animal owners don't think about the ramifications of purchasing a wild animal.

Some exotic pets are fortunate. When their owners realize they aren't able to care for them, they seek help and place the animal with an exotic-pet rescue. Unfortunately others aren't so lucky. Many die each year because their nutritional and medical needs aren't met, and others are seized by law enforcement because they're sadly neglected. As with other species, some people become collectors of exotic pets. These poor animals are often kept in deplorable conditions, and many die before law enforcement and rescue workers can intervene.

The Challenges for Exotic and Wildlife Rescues

Exotic and wildlife rescues are faced with different challenges than domestic animal rescues. For starters, not as many people understand the needs of the animals they'll have to work with, and recruiting volunteers is difficult. The unusual animals housed at these rescues attract many potential volunteers, but too often they're only interested in petting or playing with the animals—they don't really want to do the hard work of cleaning cages or building new enclosures, and are either unwilling or unable to commit the time it takes to get training on how to interact with potentially dangerous animals. In addition to this, some states and cities prohibit possession of certain species, and these rescues may need to meet USDA requirements in order to house such animals as large cats and elephants.

Before starting an exotic or wildlife rescue, determine which species you want to help. Then investigate both local and federal regulations for keeping these animals. First, check with the USDA to determine whether they have any special requirements or restrictions for people who house or own the species you will be rescuing. In some instances, you may need a license, and the USDA may insist on inspecting your facilities periodically.

Next, check with your state, county, and city governments to determine what type of restrictions they impose on those who wish to house exotic animals or wildlife. Some areas prohibit certain species, while others restrict the number of exotic animals or wildlife that may be kept. Your local government may require you to obtain a permit or may insist on inspecting your facility. If you fail to adhere to local or federal regulations, your rescue could be shut down by the authorities and you might face criminal charges or large fines. Even

Words from the Wise

Lori Runzo, of J & L Farm in Pennsylvania, says the biggest difference she's seen between their exotic and wildlife rescue and those for domestic species is that there are more laws and ordinances governing how exotic animals and wildlife are cared for. She cautions potential exotic animal and wildlife rescuers to consider the cost of rescuing these species.

"Taking in a cute baby deer is great," she adds, "but remember that when it's grown up, it'll need a 10-foot-high fence, plenty of room to run, grain, shelter, and medical care. Or consider what's involved in rescuing a mountain lion. This animal will require pounds of chicken each day, and will need a very secure cage. It isn't cheap to do this."

worse, the authorities could confiscate all your animals and euthanize them.

Costly facilities to house your animals, and large amounts of food that may be hard to find and expensive, are just the beginning of your financial concerns. You'll also need money to pay for permit fees and increased liability insurance.

Depending on the size of your animals, you may need a custom-made vehicle to transport them. And you'll quickly discover that veterinarians who treat exotic animals and wildlife are not only hard to find, but also more expensive than those who treat domestic animals. Other considerations include:

- **How much do you really know about the animals you want to rescue?** You'll need to become an expert in the care and handling of each species your rescue will house. You'll be responsible for meeting their nutritional, physical, and social needs, and you'll need to know how to safely handle and house them.

   In addition to reading books, articles, and research on your chosen species, you should talk to veterinarians, trainers, and behaviorists that currently work with the type of animal(s) you wish to rescue. If possible, visit their facilities, and inquire about internship programs. Talk to other rescuers that care for the same species, and see if you can tour their facilities or volunteer with them.

   Even after you've started your own organization, maintain relationships with these rescuers and professionals, and continue reading recent research and articles so you're constantly learning about improved techniques for feeding, housing, and handling your animals.

- **Can you meet the housing requirements for the species you want to rescue?** While small animals may not need large cages, they still need adequate space to meet their needs, as the best housing strives to mimic the animals' natural habitat. For instance, if you'll be rescuing sugar gliders, you'll need to provide places for them to climb and hide, and room to jump and glide. Reptiles need warm enclosures with pools of water, along with plants and rocks to hide under.

Large animals need space—perhaps hundreds of acres. Buffalo need plenty of room in which to roam and graze, and strong fences to contain them because they're easily startled and prone to running through fences. Deer, antelope, mustangs, and zebras need fences at least six feet tall so they can't jump over them. Large cats, wolves, bears, and other dangerous animals need large enclosures that provide adequate space to move around, but are sturdy enough to safely contain them.

You'll also need to consider the animals' social structure when planning for their housing needs. Some animals, such as mustangs, have a strong need for social interaction with other members of their species. Without that companionship, these horses can lose weight, and become lethargic and depressed. They may spend their time pacing the fence, and even calling for their own kind.

Other animals are territorial and fight when kept too close together. This tends to be a problem mostly between males, especially if there are females nearby. Some animals can share habitats with other species, while others will kill each other or compete for food if they're housed in the same habitat.

- **Can you provide the necessary security for wildlife and exotic animals?**
Since you may be housing dangerous animals, your facility needs to be well-built. Remember, if any of your animals escape and hurt other animals—or, God forbid, humans—you could be held liable for criminal negligence.

Unfortunately, exotic animals and wildlife also need protection from those who would try to get into your rescue when you're not there. If someone gets hurt by one of your animals, even after breaking into your facility, your organization could be sued. There are people who may want to let the animals go free, or steal one of them, or even hurt them. Good fencing, locked gates, surveillance, and a security system will help keep out "thrill-seekers" that want to get a peek at the "wild animals," as well as those who would hurt them or set them free.

- **Can you afford to properly feed the species you want to rescue?** Large animals, such as elephants, require a lot of food each day; grazing mammals, such as buffalo, deer, or zebra, need plentiful grass, and high-quality hay and grain when their pasture grass dies. Some exotic reptiles eat live mice or rats, and carnivorous animals, such as lions or tigers, consume large amounts of fresh meat. You need to determine:
    - Will the food you need be available?
    - Can you stomach feeding fresh meat or live animals to those animals that need it?
    - Can you afford enough food to meet the animals' needs?

- **Can you manage the rescue with limited help?** Recruiting and training volunteers is often more difficult for exotic and wildlife rescues. While many people are willing to volunteer when they hear you have exotic animals and wildlife in your rescue, they're often more interested in interacting with them than feeding or cleaning up after them. It's not unusual for volunteers to leave when they learn that they won't be handling the animals. However, you have a responsibility to keep both your animals and the public safe, so limiting volunteer contact with potentially dangerous animals should be a priority.

If you must allow volunteers to handle the animals, screen them carefully and provide comprehensive training. Select mature individuals who have been with your organization for awhile—the ones who consistently show up on time and don't complain about doing dirty work. Choose volunteers

who follow instructions and don't constantly question your rules. Your training program should include:
- A copy of rules and policies on handling the animals
- Information on how to safely handle the animals
- A description of the animals' normal behavior—including predatory behavior and signs of aggression
- Facts about zoonotic diseases and sanitation
- Emergency procedures in the event someone is injured, an animal is ill, or an animal escapes.

■ **Can you afford liability insurance?** This type of insurance is a concern for exotic-animal and wildlife rescuers. Very few insurers are willing to write policies for rescue groups—especially ones that house potentially dangerous animals. Unfortunately, in our litigious society insurance is a must—so spend time talking to insurance companies until you find one willing to write a policy for your rescue. Expect to pay high annual premiums, and to have your insurance company place restrictions on your rescue. For example, your insurance agency may insist that any volunteers who handle your animals sign a liability waiver and attend a training session. They also may insist that you limit visitors to certain areas, or that you not take your animals on educational trips to local schools.

■ **Do you know about all the zoonotic diseases that your animals could carry?** These diseases—which are spread from animals to humans—are discussed in detail in Chapter 15 (on page 185). Each species carries different diseases, and new diseases are constantly emerging. Check with your doctor, agriculture department, and the CDC for a list of possible zoonotic diseases and their symptoms. Since all mammals can contract rabies, talk to your doctor about getting a rabies vaccine. Since many fur-covered animals can carry ringworm, mange, or scabies, always carefully wash your hands and any exposed skin after handling a new animal, or one that appears to be infected with a skin disease. To further help prevent the spread of disease, keep your facility clean, washing your hands and changing clothes before you leave, and never eat or drink around the animals. All new animals should be quarantined until a veterinarian has examined them and given them a bill of clean health.

Animal rescue presents a host of challenges regardless of the species you choose to help. You need to raise money to pay for the facility and its maintenance, food for the animals, and veterinary bills. You need to work with law enforcement to help protect the animals in your community. And your organization will need to promote your activities and hold successful fund-raisers. However, exotic-animal and wildlife rescuers face unique challenges when they begin taking in unusual species. The costs for veterinary services, housing, food, and insurance is often much higher, and they risk injury when handling hurt or abused animals that are undomesticated or haven't learned to trust human caretakers.

Exotic and wildlife rescue isn't for everyone, and anyone thinking about starting a rescue of this type should do extensive research before taking the plunge. But if you're prepared for it, the rescue of both exotic animals and wildlife can be fascinating and rewarding.

The Author's Story

My Personal Experience

I decided to form a rescue because of a horse named Flight. I'd known about rescue and horse slaughter since I was a youngster. At age 12, I began taking riding lessons and soon decided that eventually I wanted my own lesson barn. My plan: to purchase all my horses at local auctions and retrain them for use as school horses. Then when a child's parents wanted to buy her a horse, I would sell them one of my retrained horses, and head back to the auction to save another.

A few years later, while I was in high school, I became a member of the Colorado Horse Rescue and corresponded with several other rescues. When I was 18, I saved my first horse. He was a teenaged, Arabian gelding named Essault, who'd been shown successfully in Arabian shows on both the regional and national level in his younger days. His owners had lost interest in him and left him in a pasture where he was slowly starving. When I bought "Aussie," he was emaciated and needed rehabilitation before I could begin working with him. I knew nothing about rehabilitating a horse, but Aussie quickly gained weight and blossomed into a beautiful, healthy specimen.

During college, I found Aussie a new home and stopped riding for a few years. After graduating, I moved to Texas and got involved with horses again. Someone told me about an older woman who needed help caring for her Arabian horses. While the place wasn't as clean as I would've liked, the horses all appeared well-fed, and I happily began helping in exchange for a horse—a gray gelding named Flight, with whom I'd fallen in love.

Unfortunately, as time went on, it became clear the woman was unable to care for all of her horses, and when she lost her land, I had to move. I was ready

The Author's Story

to take Flight with me, but she refused to let him leave the property. Since we had no written contract, there was nothing I could do. I had to leave without Flight.

About a year later, I learned that law enforcement had removed all the animals from her care shortly after I left. However, the judge who heard her case returned them to her. She immediately moved to another county. And when that county began to investigate her, she moved again. She moved at least one more time before her animals were finally seized. An investigation began after the sheriff's office received reports of a dead horse. Although I didn't know it at the time, that horse was Flight. He had become ill, and instead of treating him, she chose to euthanize him herself by administering a fatal dose of phenobarbital. She then left his body lying in front of the horse trailer in which she lived.

When I found out the horses had been seized, I called the sheriff's office. All the horses were very special to me, and I hoped that Flight would be among them. The dispatcher informed me they would be sold at auction. I used the Internet to research Texas laws governing animals seized due to abuse or neglect. I found the Texas Statutes, Health and Safety Code, Title 10: Health and Safety of Animals, Chapter 821: Treatment and disposition of animals. The law stated that if a judge determined that seized animals had been cruelly treated by their owners prior to being seized, he had three options: (1) Euthanize the animals; (2) Order the animals to public auction; or 3) Place the animals with a nonprofit organization dedicated to the welfare of animals.

Because many of these horses had received such little handling, I feared that slaughterhouse buyers would be the only people bidding on them if they were sent to auction. I began looking for an equine rescue group that could help them, but I couldn't find an active group in Texas. However, I met many other Texas equine enthusiasts online, and we all agreed that we needed an equine rescue, and in the fall of 1998, we founded Lone Star Equine Rescue, Inc.

I continue to do rescue in memory of Flight, the horse I couldn't save.

Appendices

Bluebonnet Equine Humane Society, Inc.
P O Box 15
Rosharon, TX 77583-0015
(888)542 5163
www.bluebonnetequine.org

Appendix 1: Bluebonnet Equine Humane Society Adoption Policy

Policy and Procedures Manual

Adoption Policy
Effective: June 1, 2006

Policy Number 20
Version 3.0

Policy
Bluebonnet Equine Humane Society, Inc.'s (BEHS) policy is to adopt out the equines belonging to BEHS to approved homes.

Procedure
In order to adopt, an individual or family must:
    1) Be a current member of BEHS in good standing.
    2) Have a signed liability waiver on file with BEHS.
    3) Submit a complete Adoption Application.

Once all of the above paperwork is received by BEHS, the rescue may:
    1) Review the adoption application to insure that applicant meet fostering requirements.
    2) Call and verify references.
    3) Conduct a background check.
    4) Assign a volunteer inspector to set up a time for a pre-adoption home visit. During the pre-adoption home visit, the inspector will view and photograph the property where any adopted equine(s) will live, view and photograph other equines on the property, and answer questions about the adoption process.

Throughout the adoption process (starting when an application is received), an Adoption Counselor will make periodic contact with the applicant. The Adoption Counselor will:
    • Contact the applicant when any part of the adoption application is received to give the applicant a report on the status of their application including what paperwork is outstanding.
    • Answer questions about the adoption process.
    • After a volunteer inspector has been assigned to conduct the inspection, the Adoption Counselor will check in with the applicant to insure that they've heard from the volunteer inspector.
    • Review the adoption policies and contract with the adopter.
    • Remain a point of contact for the adopter.

The volunteer inspector will submit the Inspection Worksheet and photographs to the Vice President – Equine Coordinator who will decide whether or not the prospective adoptive home meets the minimum standards of care (outlined in the Minimum Standards of Care Policy) necessary to become an adoptive home.
Either the VP-EC or AAC may refuse an adoption for any reason.

Bluebonnet Equine Humane Society, Inc.
P O Box 15
Rosharon, TX 77583-0015
(888)542 5163
www.bluebonnetequine.org

After reviewing the Inspection Worksheet and photographs, either the Vice President – Equine Coordinator (VP – EC) or the Assistant Adoption Home Coordinator (AAC) will contact the applicant.
- If the application is not approved, the VP-EC or AAC will discuss the reasons the application was not approved and outline what the applicant must do in order to be approved.
- If the application is approved, the VP-EC or AAC will notify the applicant and determine which equine(s) the adopter is interested in visiting. The AAC will put the adopter in contact with the foster home for those equines. The adopter will have two weeks to visit the equine, decide whether or not he/she will adopt, and arrange transportation of the equine. After the two week time period, the next approved applicant in line for that equine may get the opportunity to adopt him/her. Extensions may be granted if the foster home is not available during the two week timeframe. If the applicant fills out an adoption contact and pays the adoption fee but is unable to pick up the equine within the two week time-frame, the adopter will be responsible for paying board to the foster home at the rate of $50/week.

An applicant who has not been approved may file an appeal in writing to the Board of Directors within seven (7) days of receiving notice that they were not approved, and the Board of Directors will discuss the appeal. The Board of Directors has final discretion in upholding a refused adoption.

When the applicant visits the equine(s) he/she wishes to adopt if the equine is ridable, he/she and any family members who will be riding the equine once he/she is adopted must ride the equine under the supervision of the foster home. All equines must be handled by the applicant under the supervision of the foster home.

If the foster home does not feel confident that the applicant can safely and easily handle the equine, the foster home can delay the adoption and request that the Board of Directors reconsider the adoption.

If the foster home feels confident that the applicant can safely and easily handle the equine, the adopter may sign an adoption contract, and pay the adoption fee.

UNDER NO CIRCUMSTANCES *may an applicant transport an equine before he/she has signed an adoption contract and paid the adoption fee.*

When adopting, the adopter signs a contract agreeing to:
- Never use the adopted equine for breeding
- Never use the adopted equine as a Embryo Transfer donor or recipient
- Never give away, sell, lease out, send to slaughter, or otherwise dispose of the equine (aside from humane euthanasia) – if the adopter cannot keep the equine, the equine must be returned to BEHS

Bluebonnet Equine Humane Society, Inc.
P O Box 15
Rosharon, TX 77583-0015
(888) 542 5163
www.bluebonnetequine.org

- Advise BEHS if the equine is moved from the location described on the adoption contract
- Notify BEHS if the equine dies or is euthanized
- Maintain the equine in proper condition and health in accordance with the BEHS Minimum Standards of Care Policy
- Agrees to give BEHS volunteers who are acting upon instructions from the Board of Directors, Officers, or the Adoption Follow Up Coordinator access to the equine, with or without notice, in order to verify the equine's condition and health
- Immediately notify BEHS if he/she receives a citation for any criminal or civil offense related to animal abuse or neglect
- Indemnify and hold harmless BEHS, its officers, directors, members, and volunteers for any damage to property or persons caused by the equine(s) adopted from BEHS
- Pay all attorney fees, legal expenses, and court costs of BEHS incurred in connection with enforcement of the Adoption Contract
- Knowingly and voluntarily assume all risks associated with the adopted equine – including but not limited to inherent risks and risks of negligence

BEHS will maintain ownership of the adopted equine for two (2) years. During this time, BEHS will conduct the following post-adoption follow-up inspections:
- One to two (1 – 2) months after the date of the adoption contract
- Four to seven (4 – 7) months after the date of the adoption contract
- Eleven to thirteen (11 – 13) months after the date of the adoption contract
- Twenty-three to twenty-five (23 – 25) months after the date of the adoption contract
- Additionally as needed

After completion of the above requirements, BEHS will transfer ownership of the equine to the adopter. The adopter must sign and submit an adoption finalizing contract in which he/she agrees to never sell, give away, send to slaughter, or otherwise dispose of (aside from humane euthanasia) the equine adopted from BEHS. If the adopter cannot keep the equine, he/she must return the equine to BEHS. The adopter also agrees to never breed the adopted equine, and to provide follow-up reports to BEHS as necessary.

The adopter agrees to submit the following photographs three (3), four (4), and five (5) years after the date of the adoption contract:
- Front view
- Back view
- Left side view
- Right side view

At five (5) years after the date of the adoption contract, the adopter agrees to submit a Veterinary Evaluation Form and copy of the current coggins test in addition to the above photos.

Bluebonnet Equine Humane Society, Inc.
P O Box 15
Rosharon, TX 77583-0015
(888) 542 5163
www.bluebonnetequine.org

Appendix 2: Bluebonnet Equine Humane Society Membership Application Processing SOP

Membership Application Processing

Standard Operating Protocol

Membership applications may be received:
- At one of the BEHS Post Office Boxes
- As part of an Adoption Application
- As part of a Foster Application
- In person at a booth
- In person at a fundraiser or other event
- From a current member
- Via Paypal

Regardless of the manner in which they are received, all membership applications should be sent to the Executive Vice President immediately upon receipt.

Upon receipt of a membership application, the Executive Vice President shall log the membership information into the membership database and then assign the applicant to a volunteer from the membership committee.

If the applicant has provided an email address, the membership committee volunteer will immediately send the applicant an email to welcome him/her to the rescue and ask if the applicant would prefer to receive their New Member Kit via email or postal mail. If the applicant did not provide an email address, did not answer the email, or requested the New Member Kit by sent via postal mail, the volunteer will send a New Member Kit to the applicant via postal mail no more than five days after being assigned the applicant.

Two weeks after receipt of the new member application, a volunteer from the membership committee will call the new member to welcome him or her to the rescue, ask if he/she received the New Member Kit, invite the new member to any scheduled events or get-togethers, and see if the new member has any questions about the rescue or would like to receive more information about volunteer opportunities. If the new member would like information about particular volunteer opportunities (such as fostering, trailering, fundraising, etc.), the volunteer will pass the new member's information to the appropriate committee chairpersons.

© 2005 Bluebonnet Equine Humane Society, Inc   Adoption Policy

Bluebonnet Equine Humane Society, Inc.
P O Box 15
Rosharon, TX 77583-0015
(888) 542 5163
www.bluebonnetequine.org

Appendix 3: Sample Press Release

For Immediate Release
For more information:
Jennifer Williams, President
Email: jenn@bluebonnetequine.org
Phone: (888) 542 5163
www.bluebonnetequine.org

BLUEBONNET EQUINE HUMANE SOCIETY FORMED TO HELP HORSES IN TEXAS AND ARKANSAS

Dr. Jennifer Williams, former president and co-founder of Lone Star Equine Rescue, has partnered with horse enthusiasts across Texas and Arkansas to create Bluebonnet Equine Humane Society, Inc. (BEHS). BEHS incorporated in Texas and Arkansas in March 2005 and plans to improve the lives of equines by educating and helping owners, assisting law enforcement agencies, rehabilitating abused and neglected equines, and placing them into safe, permanent homes.

BEHS is off to a running start. Dr. Jennifer Williams, President has not only has spoken on the subject of Horse Rescue and Retirement at the American Quarter Horse Convention on March 12 in St. Louis, Missouri, where she proudly announced the formation of the organization. Then on April 19, 2005, she also spoke in an educational session preceding at the Unwanted Horse Summit in Washington DC. The summit was hosted by the American Association of Equine Practitioners (AAEP) and served as a catalyst for identifying long-term solutions designed to improve the quality of life of unwanted horses.

A large part of the "unwanted horse problem" is the large number of equines sold throughout the United States each year to one of the three slaughterhouses that process equines for human consumption. As many concerned with equine welfare debate The American Horse Slaughter Prevention Act, the horse industry has begun to address the reasons horses end up at the slaughter house.

BEHS is proud to be involved in the solution to this distressing problem by allowing owners to donate horses and other equines to the organization as an alternative to auctions and the slaughter house. Additionally, BEHS plans to work with law enforcement agencies to investigate reports of abuse and neglect and to assist officers in removing equines from neglectful homes.

page 1, C 2005 Bluebonnet Equine Humane Society, Inc   Adoption Polic

Bluebonnet Equine Humane Society, Inc.
P O Box 15
Rosharon, TX 77583-0015
(888)542 5163
www.bluebonnetequine.org

Through the use of committees, BEHS hopes to enlist the assistance and expertise of members in running the organization. A PR Committee has been formed to promote the organization, a Fundraising Committee will plan fundraisers, and Corporate Sponsorship Committee will develop a corporate sponsorship program and solicit sponsorships from Texas and Arkansas companies. Several other committees will govern other aspects of the organization's activities. Members are also encouraged to give input on the policies and procedures of the organization and to volunteer to establish new programs for the rescue.

Bluebonnet Equine Humane Society needs your help in order to help the horses and other equines who need them. Consider supporting BEHS with a financial contribution (the organization's 501(c)(3) status is pending) or by becoming a member. BEHS also needs foster homes and volunteers to help with trailering, fundraising, and PR.

For more information on BEHS, please visit http://www.bluebonnetequine.org, call (888) 542-5163, or email info@bluebonnetequine.org.

Appendix 4: List of Horse Rescues

These horse rescues were mentioned in or interviewed for this book. Being listed here is not necessarily an endorsement of the rescue's policies and practices. Anyone interested in working with any rescue organization should contact the rescue, ask for references, and review the organization's policies and procedures to ensure that they agree with how the organization operates.

Black Beauty Ranch
PO Box 367
Murchison, TX 75778
(903) 469-3811
blackbeautyinfo@fundforanimals.org
http://fundforanimals.org/ranch/

Bluebonnet Equine Humane Society
P.O. Box 15
Rosharon, TX 77583
(888) 542-5163
info@bluebonnetequine.org
http://www.bluebonnetequine.org/

Chance's Miniature Horse Rescue
Virginia St. Pierre
735 Chestnut Lane
Berryville, VA 22611
(520) 825-8086
treasurer@chancesminihorserescue.org
http://www.chancesminihorserescue.org/

Colorado Horse Rescue
10386 North 65th Street
Longmont, CO 80503
(720) 494-1414
http://www.chr.org/

Crosswinds Equine Rescue, Inc.
1476 NCR 1350 E
Tuscola, IL 61953
(217) 832-2010
http://hometown.aol.com/horses5ormore/homepage.html

Days End Farm Horse Rescue
15856 Frederick Road
Lisbon, Maryland, 21765
(301) 854-5037 or (410) 442-1564
www.defhr.org

South Carolina Awareness and Rescue for Equines
PO Box 84914
Lexington, SC 29073
(888) 866-8744
www.scequinerescue.org

Spring Hill Horse Rescue
2617 Union St.
Brandon, VT 05733
(802) 247-2857
http://www.springhillrescue.com/

Standardbred Retirement Foundation
P. O. Box 763
Freehold N.J. 07728
(732) 462-8773
srfmail1@verizon.net
http://www.adoptahorse.org/

Thoroughbred Retirement Foundation
P.O. Box 3387
Saratoga Springs, NY 12866
Phone: (518) 226-0028
http://www.trfinc.org/

Traveller's Rescue Equine Elders Sanctuary
PO Box 2260
Spotsylvania, VA 22553
(540) 972-0936
info@equineelders.org
www.equineelders.org

True Innocents Equine Rescue
7900 Limonite Ave., Ste. G, #278
Riverside, CA 92509
(951) 360-1464
info@TIERRescue.org
http://www.tierrescue.org/

United States Equine Rescue League
PO Box 352
Kernersville, NC 27285
(336) 720-9257
info@ncerl.com
http://www.ncerl.com/

Whidbey Island Rescue for Equines
1258 Silver Lake Road
Oak Harbor, WA 98277
(360) 675-9252
http://www.equusworld.net/_/rescues/

White Bird Appaloosa Horse Rescue
1688 Burke's Tavern Road
Burkeville, VA 23922
Phone: 434-767-2839
whitebirdapps@gmail.com
http://whitebirdapps.com/

Appendix 5: Henneke Body Condition Scoring Chart

Score/Condition	Neck	Withers	Loin
1. Poor – Animal extremely emaciated with no fatty tissue felt	Bone structure easily visible	Bone structure easily visible	Spinous processes project prominently
2. Very Thin – Animal emaciated	Bone structure faintly visible	Bone structure faintly visible	Slight fat covering over the base of the spinous processes. The transverse processes of lumbar vertebrae feel rounded. Spinous processes are prominent.
3. Thin	Neck accentuated	Withers accentuated	Fat buildup halfway on spinuous processes but processes still easily visible. Transverse processes cannot be felt.
4. Moderately Thin	Not obviously thin	Not obviously thin	Negative crease down back
5. Moderate	Blends smoothly into body	Rounded over spinous	Level
6. Moderately Fleshy	Fat beginning to be deposited	Fat beginning to be deposited	Possible slight positive crease down back
7. Fleshy	Fat deposited	Fat deposited	Possible positive crease down back
8. Fat – Fat deposited along buttocks	Noticeable thickening	Areas along withers filled with fat	Positive crease
9. Extremely Fat – Fat along inner buttocks may rub together. Flanks are filled in flush.	Bulging fat	Bulging fat	Obvious positive crease

Henneke Body Condition Scoring Chart, continued

Score/Condition	Tailhead	Ribs	Shoulder
1. Poor – Animal extremely emaciated with no fatty tissue felt	Tailhead bones and hook bones project prominently	Project prominently	Bone structure easily visible
2. Very Thin – Animal emaciated	Tailhead prominent	Ribs prominent	Bone structure faintly visible
3. Thin	The tailhead is prominent but the individual vertebrae cannot be visibly identified. While hook bones are rounded, they're still easily visible. Pin bones not distinguishable.	Slight fat covering over ribs but ribs still easily visible	Shoulder accentuated
4. Moderately Thin	Prominence varies with conformation, but fat can be felt around tailhead and hooks and pins not visible.	Slight fat cover over ribs but ribs are still visible	Shoulder accentuated
5. Moderate	Fat around tailhead begins to feel spongy	Not visible but can be easily felt	Blends smoothly into body
6. Moderately Fleshy	Fat around tailhead feels soft	Fat over ribs feels spongy	Fat beginning to be deposited
7. Fleshy	Fat around tailhead feels soft	Individual ribs can be felt, but fat fills between ribs	Fat deposited behind shoulder
8. Fat – Fat deposited along buttocks	Tailhead fat very soft	Difficult to feel	Area behind shoulders is flush with body
9. Extremely Fat – Fat along inner buttocks may rub together. Flanks are filled in flush.	Bulging fat	Patchy fat	Bulging fat